Classroom Talk in Practice

Teachers' Experiences of Oracy in Action

Rupert Knight

Mc Graw Hill

Open University Press

Open University Press
McGraw Hill
Unit 4,
Foundation Park
Roxborough Way
Maidenhead
SL6 3UD

email: emea_uk_ireland@mheducation.com
world wide web: www.openup.co.uk

First edition published 2022

A catalogue record of this book is available from the British Library

ISBN-13: 9780335250035
ISBN-10: 0335250033
eISBN: 9780335250042

Library of Congress Cataloging-in-Publication Data
CIP data applied for

Typeset by Transforma Pvt. Ltd., Chennai, India

Praise page

"Classroom Talk in Practice *is an essential read for anyone who wants to understand how the recent revival of interest in talk as a means of learning, and as a vital component of a rounded education, is exemplified in practice. Expertly weaving together illuminating illustrations of teachers and students talking together with lucid accounts of the research evidence base, it reveals the approaches that work successfully. For practising teachers, it offers a guide to how to exercise sound professional judgement in selecting and sustaining strategies that place talk at the centre of teaching and learning, so that all students benefit.*"

Alan Howe, Education Consultant
and Associate with Oracy Cambridge

"This thought provoking and highly informative book is a perfect handbook for teachers and school leaders interested in improving the quality of talk in their classrooms."

Amy Gaunt and Alice Stott, Directors at Voice 21
and authors of Transform Teaching and
Learning through Talk: the Oracy Imperative

"Professor Knight's book 'Classroom Talk in Practice' provides the rationale for high quality classroom talk as well as practical advice with real world examples for teachers and school leaders at all stages of their Oracy journeys. In busy schools with competing priorities, it can be tricky to know where to begin with a new initiative; this book provides easy-to-follow steps and guidance for every type of talk task, role and classroom."

Chaitan Rajania, Oracy & Curriculum Lead
at Madani Schools Federation

Contents

Acknowledgements

First and foremost, my thanks go to the anonymous school colleagues and their students who feature in this book. The source material was collected at a time of huge challenge for schools. While the content of the chapters to follow refers only in passing to the pandemic, in reality its influence pervaded education in this period. In the circumstances, I am especially grateful to all those who gave up precious time to speak to me and welcome me briefly, but wholeheartedly, into their schools. It was a real privilege to experience and learn about their practice. I would also like to thank members of the Voice 21 team who shared their expertise and knowledge of schools across the country. Finally, I am grateful to the colleagues, past and present, who have directly or indirectly helped, inspired and encouraged me in so many ways.

Introduction: starting from the practice

Aims of this book

It has always been tempting to see children's talk as innate and therefore to be taken for granted as a by-product of other learning. Almost five decades ago, when researching spoken language in classrooms was in its infancy, Connie and Harold Rosen disagreed: 'We could say that children's capacity to talk is there so that all we have to do is draw upon it appropriately just as we do their capacity to walk or to see. We could say that, but we don't.'[1] Since then, many others have come to the same conclusion as the Rosens. If classroom talk is to be purposeful and productive, it is worthy of specific attention as a focus of learning in its own right. Indeed, talk has been investigated extensively and many of the outcomes will appear in the chapters to follow.

This book is an attempt to help teachers consider some of the issues around talk in the context of their own classrooms, chiefly through that most precious and powerful of opportunities: gaining an insight into other teachers' practices in a diverse range of schools. In doing so, this book sets out to address three important questions:

1 What practices have schools found to be successful for promoting and using high-quality classroom talk?
2 What can be learned from the decision-making, experiences and processes relating to classroom talk at these schools?
3 How do these practices relate to what is known of the evidence-informed principles underlying classroom talk?

The aim, therefore, is to celebrate real classroom practice, but also to understand and learn from that practice. There are already many authoritative texts on the social constructivist and sociocultural theory that often underpins the use of classroom talk[2] and plenty of reports of the decades of research in this field.[3] However, it is a sad but well-established fact that educational theory and research often fail to have an impact on the daily realities of teachers' classroom practice. Sometimes, they seek to solve different problems from those prioritized by teachers; sometimes they generate different forms of knowledge, so that insights are not communicated in ways that link readily to practical implementation.[4] Starting with the practice is an attempt to stay grounded in the daily realities of teachers' work.

In some respects, research is becoming better connected to teachers through teacher-led, bottom-up research movements, research summaries or meta-analyses and 'what works' organizations such as the Education Endowment Foundation in the UK[5] or What Works Clearinghouse in the US.[6] However, there are questions to ask about generalizing and translating findings from large-scale trials or aggregations of diverse data.[7] For one thing, the complexity of the classroom means that any attempt to control conditions and derive universal findings in a 'scientific' way is bound to be challenging. For another, before considering 'what works' or 'effectiveness', we need to ask more fundamentally: effective for what? Education has many possible outcomes, so evaluating success always implies a value judgement about purpose and this question of purpose will be explored in Chapter 1.

Meanwhile, there also exist many useful sources of practical ideas for the classroom, often grounded in research-based principles. For all their great value, however, there is always a danger of by-passing professional judgement in the enthusiastic rush to try out an attractive activity. Despite policies that appear to set out to simplify and codify teachers' expertise, there remains a strong counter-argument that a hallmark of teacher expertise is not the mastery of a body of content but the exercise of professional judgement. A long line of educational thinkers has argued for the central importance of context-specific judgement or 'practical wisdom'[8] and, indeed, it has been argued that expert teachers do not simply know more; they *interpret and respond differently* to situations.[9]

Learning about classroom talk from practice

This book, then, is an attempt to navigate a pathway between these challenges. First and foremost, it is a book centred on exploring practices already used in schools in response to the everyday needs of learners. At its heart is evidence collected from diverse schools and age phases around England, offering real-life examples from schools and individual classrooms. It is important to clarify two points, however. First, the book does not claim to offer a representative depiction of current practice. On the contrary, school and classroom examples, drawn from observations and interviews, have been selected, not necessarily as models of practice, but on the basis of their potential for illustrating various aspects of classroom talk. Secondly, these examples have not been formally analysed with a view to generating 'findings' but are instead used predominantly as a starting point for reflection and discussion about the related issues.

To this end, rather than offering up descriptions of practice for mimicry, the examples are intended to support the reader's own exercise of professional judgement. By juxtaposing contrasting examples from different contexts, the hope is that new insights might be gained. The book attempts, wherever possible, to consider the *meaning* that lies behind the observed practice in each case. Delving beneath the surface of a taught lesson and accessing the often tacit, intuitive reasoning of teachers is notoriously difficult.[10] The aim, where

Table 1 Schools featured in this book

School pseudonym	Type of school and age range	Region of England
Underwood	Primary 3–11	South
Queensway	Primary 3–11	Midlands
Newton	Primary 3–11	Midlands
Woodham	Primary 3–11	East
Rushton	Primary 4–11	North
Downland	Primary 7–11	South
Northside	Secondary 11–16	Midlands
Larchwell	Secondary 11–16	South
Riverside	Secondary 11–18	North
Southlea	Secondary 11–18	Midlands
Brookfield	Secondary 11–18	Midlands
Fairway	Primary and Secondary 4–16	North
Eastland	Primary and Secondary 4–18	South

possible, is therefore to expose something of the rationales and the journeys that underpin teachers' use of talk in classrooms. As Robin Alexander wrote in his influential study of classrooms across cultures: 'we must talk with those whom we watch.'[11] There is also an attempt in the analysis to go beyond the *'what'* and the *'how'* to the *'why'* of the observed practice by making connections from specific school contexts to what is known more generally about classroom talk so that highly situated examples are linked to some of the broader, underlying principles in this field. In summary, therefore, the aim of discussing each example of practice is to address four questions:

1 What is going on in this example?
2 What is the meaning underlying this example?
3 How does this meaning relate to what we know more broadly?
4 What are the implications of this example for teachers' practice?

While the schools, teachers and students have been anonymized with pseudonyms, the practice documented here is authentic and is, with one exception, based on interviews and observations undertaken between late 2020 and early 2022. Within the constraints of maintaining anonymity by minimizing identifying features, the broad profiles of the 13 schools featured in this book are summarized in Table 1.

Finally, a word on terminology: while learners in classrooms are described in various ways, often depending on age phase or country ('pupils', 'students', 'young people', etc.), this book refers to 'students' throughout, as a catch-all term that seems to span contexts most neatly.

Organization of the rest of this book

Chapter 1 begins by considering a variety of perspectives on, and arguments for, classroom talk and introduces the concept of oracy. A frequent criticism levelled at the use of evidence in education is that it is insufficiently cumulative, as too little attention is paid to what has come before. With that in mind, **Chapter 2** attempts to establish common reference points by taking stock of what is already known about powerful ways of putting talk into practice. Having established these basic principles and practices surrounding classroom talk, **Chapters 3** to **8** provide in-depth examples and analysis from the school observations and interviews. These themed chapters begin with brief insights from theory to frame the practice. They then comprise lesson excerpts, insights into teachers' judgements and decision-making, commentaries and links to wider knowledge of the field. The chapters encompass learning to and through talk in small groups, whole classes and beyond and they span primary and secondary age phases. Material in each chapter is drawn from a range of schools, allowing for comparisons and contrasts to be explored. Woven into this coverage is consideration of important issues such as the role of technology, making talk inclusive and subject and age variations. The book concludes, in **Chapter 9**, by briefly drawing together the common themes and lessons learned.

1 Making the case for classroom talk

Chapter preview

Beginning with an episode of classroom practice, Chapter 1 makes the case for a study of children's talk, exploring questions that might be raised. The argument draws on three key perspectives, related to different – though over-lapping – aims of education. The concept of oracy is introduced and critiqued. The chapter covers:

- Starting with the practice: exploring classroom talk using different perspectives
- Making the case for classroom talk: three broad arguments
- Introducing the concept of oracy

Starting with the practice: exploring classroom talk using different perspectives

The premise of this book is that focusing on and deconstructing examples of authentic classroom practice is a valuable learning experience. Without delay, therefore, let's get straight into a lesson and meet Year 6 on a Friday morning at Underwood Primary School.

Classroom example: character discussion in English

'Who can show me an action for the word "modest"?'

Year 6 students have been studying *The Wind in the Willows* and are considering extracts from the text which reveal characters' attributes. The process involves engaging with some unfamiliar vocabulary. Their teacher, Richard, begins by exploring each term, bringing words such as 'vacilla-tory' and 'impulsive' to life through drama and collective rehearsal of pronunciation.

Armed with the vocabulary, trios of students start to debate which adjective best describes Toad in this story. This debate centres on a large sheet offering four possibilities to choose from. When a student is ready to share an idea, they indicate their readiness to be the instigator by putting their thumb up for others to see. As their argument is shared, a counter is placed on the sheet to represent the turn they have taken.

After a few minutes of vigorous group discussion, a child is invited to make the case to the whole class for the most fitting adjective. Richard listens but then gently offers an alternative view, explaining that he is in the role of a challenger. He notes a student in one group who has changed his mind during the discussion, due to the persuasive case made by a peer. Having modelled in this way, Richard encourages others to contribute: 'Who wants to build or challenge now?' As ideas are offered, they are evaluated collectively for clarity and their use of evidence to support the argument. Eventually, students are asked to return briefly to their small groups to seek a consensus based on all that they have heard. Some groups reach agreement, but others do not.

The discussion now turns to a provocative question requiring students to draw on a wide range of evidence from the text: 'Does Toad deserve his 20-year prison sentence?' On the screen and on students' sheets is an image of weighing scales. Children will be placing tokens on one side or other of the balance as they discuss and 'weigh' the evidence. For some children, actual scales are used, allowing them to see how the balance is shifted by the number of arguments for and against. This time, a new skill is highlighted: probing. An icon for probing – part of a set seen in every classroom – is displayed and Richard pauses to consider what this means in practice. He invites an example of a limited response to the question that might need elaboration and then sets about modelling a probe for further information. The students' sheet reinforces this move by providing relevant sentence stems. As the children begin to consider the question, there is the sound of lively discussion and disagreement, with every answer now drawing on evidence from the text extracts provided.

This is a brief episode from a lesson in one classroom, within a particular school. Nevertheless, if we delve beneath the surface, there is a great deal to enjoy and examine here. With a focus on spoken language, this extract can be explored from a number of perspectives by asking three preliminary questions which frame the classroom examples throughout this book.

1 *Why are students talking?* This is talk with a clear purpose, as students use evidence from a text to make inferences about characters. Discussing the text allows for an initial oral rehearsal of ideas, free from the constraints of formal written recording. However, this is not merely the rehearsal of 'correct' answers or the sharing of unconnected, individual views. The structure of this lesson promotes the consideration of diverse but interconnected

views so that the understanding of the text is collaboratively constructed in small groups and as a class.

2 *How are students talking?* The purposeful collaboration and collective building of ideas in evidence here is no accident. Students are provided with concrete, visual and spoken tools to aid their discussions, while their modes of interaction are valued, explicitly modelled and noted as objects of learning in their own right, alongside the comprehension outcomes. These structures are familiar to the children and appear to be the part of a long-established shared understanding about classroom practices.

3 *Who is talking and to whom?* This is a lesson in which every student has a voice and an audience. The use of small group roles and tokens, as well as deliberately open-ended stimuli provoking disagreement, means that participation is designed into the tasks. This is not, however, an exercise in eliciting minimal responses from as many students as possible: group talk is of a high quality and students represent and interact with their peers' views. All of this means that participation involves legitimizing and valuing students' authentic voices.

These three questions relate to the *purpose, form* and *participation* associated with classroom talk. In the chapters to follow, these themes will be helpful in understanding the underlying values and principles behind the practice. But first let's pause and consider the case for a focus on classroom talk. After all, it is just one element of a complex educational ecosystem.

Three broad arguments for classroom talk

The introduction to the book referred to exploring 'successful' talk practices, but any judgement of success depends fundamentally on clarity about different types of educational outcome. At the risk of over-simplifying, it might be helpful to think of three key, evidence-informed arguments, or three forms of 'success', where talk is concerned:

1 The communicative competence, or skill for life, argument.
2 The cognitive, or vehicle for learning, argument.
3 The student voice, or participatory, argument.

In each case, the argument is related back to the Year 6 lesson at Underwood and comments from a teacher in one of the other schools further illustrate the case being made.

1. The communicative competence argument

Communicative competence concerns an individual's capability not only to use spoken language but also to apply it appropriately in social situations.[1] A long line of research, particularly from the 1970s onwards, makes the case for a strong link between spoken language proficiency and wider outcomes, both in school and in life after formal education. The Confederation of British Industry, in its depiction of work-readiness, for example, refers explicitly to communication skills, including public speaking.[2] Conversely, early problems with the use of spoken language, commonly referred to as speech, language and communication needs (SLCN), have been found to be strongly associated not only with later academic attainment, but also mental health difficulties and involvement in the criminal justice system.[3] Not only are such SLCN more prominent in children from economically disadvantaged backgrounds, but this social divide is also evident more generally in the differing vocabulary test results between these groups.[4]

Quite apart from the accomplished everyday use of speech, competence more specifically with certain registers of language is also associated with the idea of cultural capital, discussed in Box 1 below. While acknowledging these issues, it is important, however, to avoid adopting a purely deficit view. Children often bring to the classroom many assets, or 'funds of knowledge',[5] from their home lives and the problem is sometimes one of a mismatch between the expectations and registers of language use in their communities and in their classrooms.[6] As will be discussed later, consensus over what constitutes 'good' spoken language is far from straightforward.

Box 1

Theory in focus: cultural capital

Cultural capital has become a much-discussed subject in education. For example, in England, it merits a dedicated section within the latest school inspection framework.[7] This definition, however, is based in turn on a passage from the English National Curriculum referring to *'the essential knowledge that pupils need to be educated citizens'*.[8] Cultural capital here seems to have been very narrowly defined as knowledge, in contrast to the much broader vision of the concept's originator, Pierre Bourdieu.[9]

Bourdieu's exploration of structures and divisions within society led him to identify cultural capital, alongside economic and social capital, as a major determinant of one's position within the social order. Cultural capital, he suggested, is displayed in a person's dispositions and habits, in their material possessions and is ultimately validated through academic qualifications. Depending on what is valued by a particular society, these indicators of background and class may advantage or disadvantage an individual.

Rather than a limited focus on a body of approved knowledge (which is bound to be contested) within a curriculum, Bourdieu's original conception suggests that behaviours and skills are also likely to be important for social mobility. This implies an important place for spoken language. The challenge, however, is going beyond merely mimicking superficially 'sophisticated' forms of talk and instead learning to use language to convey learners' more authentic intellectual and cultural assets.

Relating this argument to Richard's Year 6 classroom from the start of the chapter, our attention might be drawn to the ways in which communicative competence and confidence – and thereby cultural capital – were being developed. We saw this in the modelling and use of ambitious vocabulary and precise sentence structures, as well as through the attention given to appropriate forms of interaction, such as ways of politely disagreeing with views. At the same time, we might note that, while certain structures are provided, talk was not being 'policed' or corrected, as it was acknowledged that the mode was one of reasoning rather than formal presentation.

School example: confident communicators

At Riverside, a teacher singles out building students' confidence as effective communicators for life as a prime motivation for their focus on talk:

'For me, it's about developing the confidence of young people, giving them the tools to articulate themselves and to go out into the world and hold their own, basically ... We're a diverse school and I have some girls who never really spoke at all and now they are some of my best debaters. They've found their voice, they've found who they are and that's amazing because these are the kids who don't necessarily have some of the options to do that ... I had an email from a girl who said, "I'm not going to get anywhere in life if I don't talk". Seeing that is brilliant – going forward, people who didn't get the chance are going to get that chance.

If you teach them how to speak correctly, then people listen to them ... Now when someone says something really well, it's getting them respect and a platform. There's a culture in some of our classrooms where if you answer a question well, everyone's really proud of you.'

Enhancing life opportunities is at the forefront of this example and the reference to speaking 'correctly' raises interesting questions about the forms of talk that are privileged, an issue to be considered in Chapter 3.

2. The cognitive argument

As well as spoken language being a valid educational goal in its own right, it is also a powerful vehicle for learning across the curriculum. Learning in a school context is an inherently social activity and talk is a powerful medium for understanding. There is good evidence for the impact of talk on many forms of attainment. For example, recent large-scale studies have associated particular aspects of productive dialogue with subsequent attainment gains in assessments of English and mathematics.[10] However, this benefit is not simply about an improved command of language improving literacy skills and thereby unlocking attainment across the wider curriculum. The impact is also to be found in improvements to thinking and understanding. Studies have, for example, found high-quality peer talk to be related to improvements in reasoning and problem-solving.[11] Box 2 illustrates the ways that this kind of talk can make a difference: not only to immediate learning as a group, but also to later individual outcomes. Two key points arising from such studies are firstly that gains are often sustainable and transferable to new contexts, but also that they are dependent on the quality and nature of the talk involved. The question of what constitutes *productive* talk and how it might be achieved is by no means straightforward but will be a focus of the analysis of practice in the chapters to follow.

Box 2

Theory in focus: interthinking

Chapter 5 will look in more depth at the nature of and conditions for 'exploratory talk' between peers. In terms of making the cognitive case for productive talk between students, however, the insights of Neil Mercer and colleagues are of great interest, particularly in considering how working collectively yields later, transferable benefits for the *individual*.[12] Mercer identifies three ways that such talk enhances learning:

1 At a straightforward level, there is an element of 'appropriation'. Other students may have knowledge or strategies that can simply be transmitted and picked up.
2 A stronger argument is 'co-construction'. By considering alternative perspectives and collectively reasoning, a group may come to an outcome that is more than the sum of its parts. These new understandings or strategies can then be applied by an individual to other situations.
3 Finally, and perhaps most powerfully, there is also a process of 'transformation'. Transformation refers to the way that dialogue leads to a greater critical, metacognitive awareness of the very process of weighing up different arguments, reasoning and problem-solving. Collaboration brings often-implicit reasoning strategies out into the open explicitly, with the result that these processes can be internalized and later used independently at an individual level.

Mercer's work reminds us that there can be many forms of end point: not always a product or solution but sometimes transformative metacognitive learning related to new habits of thinking.

Revisiting Richard's Year 6 classroom, there were hints of positive learning outcomes from this sort of peer-to-peer talk. Discussion tasks had been carefully engineered to encourage the sharing of different perspectives through building and challenging, while the quest for consensus in groups was likely to enhance the skilled reasoning and deliberation. There was also evidence in the extract of one student changing his mind as a result of his group's discussion – perhaps an indicator of the co-construction referred to in Box 2. What was also clear, however, was that this learning was built upon firm foundations in the form of classroom culture and procedures for talking.

School example: collaborative dialogue

A teacher at Brookfield reflects on how productive talk between peers is at the heart of mathematics teaching:

'We look closely at the seating plan so we pair people of different, but close, attainment so they can help one another. Then we choose problems that are deliberately ambiguous so there will be more of a discussion. It's not just an easy right or wrong answer: it's a rich task with low access, high ceiling. We start off with something they can all discuss and collaborate on, so some students will naturally get there a bit quicker and start helping others, but then it will inevitably be ramped up in difficulty ... It helps the lower attaining students by them being exposed to how other students behave and act in that maths environment. It's more powerful than anything else we do ... Every child uses a mini whiteboard and we always work with group tables so it's conducive to that style of lesson. As a team, we did an exercise, visualizing the kind of lessons we wanted and we were all pretty much the same: noisy but productive.'

This teacher has come to realize the cognitive value of 'messy' exploratory talk as a learning process, alongside more polished forms of talk for a wider audience. Crucially, this is an inclusive process for *all* students.

3. The student voice argument

Teaching students to articulate their ideas and reasoning goes beyond an interest in skills or attainment. A commitment to listening to and valuing diverse perspectives is also a commitment to a vision of education as a collective, empowering endeavour. In fact, a student's right to be heard is enshrined in the UN's Rights of the Child, which include the right to express views and have them taken seriously.[13] *Taken alone*, some teacher-dominated forms of classroom discourse might be seen as limited preparation for participation in democratic society in their promotion of a narrow, uncritical acceptance of knowledge and authority and their potential marginalization of some groups in the classroom.[14] While teacher-led episodes within lessons are an essential and often efficient means of communicating new knowledge, they do not constitute the entirety of learning. The voices and interests of the learners also play an important role.

Beyond these ongoing principles of democratic involvement in one's own education, student voice has more recently assumed an enhanced status. Arising from the pandemic of 2020 onwards, an even greater emphasis has been placed on the affective aspects of talk, for example in guidance from the

Mental Health Foundation in the UK[15] which emphasizes the need for allowing time for young people to talk through their experiences as they return to school. Meanwhile, in the face of debate about 'fake news' and 'post-truth', Alexander has argued for the heightened importance of teaching students how to use dialogue in an accountable, reasoned way.[16] Student voice and participation must, however, be promoted in an authentic way, as discussed in Box 3 below.

Box 3

Theory in focus: dialogue and democracy

Striking a balance between purposeful learning and students' authentic involvement in their learning is not easy. Alitza Segal and Adam Lefstein's work in Israeli classrooms[17] shows how, all too often, what seems to be dialogue amounts only to 'exuberant voiceless participation', in which students are talking but mainly articulating the teacher's viewpoint.

Segal and Lefstein propose four conditions for nurturing authentic and unofficial voices:

1 *Having the opportunity to speak* may involve getting beyond the constraints and norms of the classroom which tend to limit voices.
2 *Speaking one's own ideas* depends on positioning the official (often teacher) perspective as one of many.
3 *Speaking on one's own terms* means sometimes allowing for informal, non-standard forms of expression.
4 *Being heeded* involves others listening to and building on a contribution.

In all of this, however, there are tensions to be resolved as, for example, teachers seek to reconcile the principle of co-constructed knowledge with the realities of the official knowledge at the heart of the lesson content. Segal and Lefstein refer to 'making space' for unofficial voices, so the question for schools like Woodham, below, may be to consider where in the curriculum and beyond these spaces may legitimately exist and where the official voice prevails.

In Richard's Year 6 lesson, we saw some of the hallmarks of authentic voices and participation. Students were given an opportunity to rehearse ideas initially within the safety of a small group and, when they were shared more widely, Richard opened the floor to a range of viewpoints. Arguments were evaluated less for correctness than for the quality of reasoning and communication. The use in small groups of tokens for talk helped to ensure that debate was not dominated by a few voices and that there was an expectation of participation by all. The importance, mentioned in Box 3, of being heeded is very much in evidence, as teacher and students built on one another's contributions.

School example: giving children a voice

At Woodham, teachers recognize the way that giving talk high status helps to ensure children have a voice, not only for their academic progress but also their wider development:

'One of the many things that [oracy] has done is really give the children a voice in the classroom and has convinced teachers to take a step back. We work really hard on pupils working harder than the teachers and teachers saying less than the pupils and we've reaped the benefits of that.

Instead of a school council, every child is in a mixed age circle group of 30 and every teacher and LSA is responsible, so everybody has a say. The children have a voice in the way that things happen.

I've seen a shift in children being able to talk about their feelings and problems more now. If I ask a child, "Why are you feeling like this?" or "What has happened?", they are able to really think about it and structure their thoughts. It's not just having a conversation, making a first impression, giving a presentation, having a job interview, it's about their emotional and mental wellbeing. They're able to think in this same structured way as well.'

There is a mention here of teachers stepping back and allowing a greater emphasis on student voice. This has implications for the teacher's role in the classroom, something explored particularly in Chapters 4, 5, and 6.

Introducing the concept of oracy

To help set up the chapters to follow and to determine the scope of this topic, this is a good place to introduce the concept of oracy. Oracy is usually attributed to the work of Andrew Wilkinson,[18] who attempted to capture proficiency in spoken language (including listening), and elevate its status as a fundamental skill, alongside the likes of literacy and numeracy. While this original view aligns with the first of our arguments above – spoken language as a skill in its own right – more recent interpretations have also emphasized the second: what might be referred to as 'oral pedagogy'. In this broader sense, oracy, therefore, has been characterized by Voice 21 as the intersection of these two goals, as suggested by Figure 1 below.

A renewed focus on oracy is highlighted in the UK, for example, through national campaigning and training from charitable organizations such as Voice 21 and the English Speaking Union[19] and was foregrounded by the Oracy All Party Parliamentary Group (APPG) and its report in 2021.[20] For all its potential as a concept with increasingly common currency, oracy as a specific term has drifted in and out of use since its 1960s origins (see, for example, its brief prominence in the late 1980s and early 1990s with the National Oracy Project[21]).

Figure 1 Oracy as the intersection of learning to talk and learning through talk.[22]

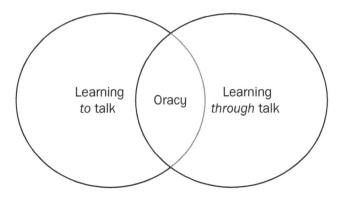

Even now, it is clear that the domains in Figure 1 cover hugely diverse activities with varying degrees of overlap, so the term necessarily remains somewhat ill-defined and has historically been used mainly in the UK (though 'orality' as a way of more generally denoting a culture of oral communication, in contrast to written, has been used more widely[23]). For these reasons, while aligning with the broader definition above and citing the term frequently, this book refers by default to 'classroom talk' more generally.

Nevertheless, Figure 1 also allows consideration of the forms of talk which might be located *outside* the two circles shown here. To begin with, this book's main focus is on *students'* spoken language. Teacher talk, in the form of explaining, modelling and so on, is an essential feature of any classroom but is referred to here where it provides a stimulus for student talk, as in the case of questioning, for example. Student talk, more specifically, sometimes involves informal, social interaction. While this can often be rich in meaning-making, the focus here is on the intentional use of *talk for learning*. Finally, students come to school from varied home environments that may frequently be rich in oral language and, while the question of comparing communities' linguistic codes with the forms of talk valued in the classroom is a focus of study in its own right, it is touched on only briefly. To summarize, then, this book is about largely planned-for student talk within the school context with the goal of communicating effectively, but also of thinking and jointly constructing understanding.

Questions for reflection

- Choose an episode in your own classroom and consider the opening three questions. Why are students talking? How are they talking? Who is talking and to whom?

- Of the arguments outlined in this chapter for promoting classroom talk, which is the most persuasive for you? Does this depend on a school's context?
- To what extent might the concept of oracy, as presented in this chapter, help a teacher to think about classroom talk?

Related resources

- The Oracy All Party Parliamentary Group (APPG) website has details on the Speak for Change Inquiry and includes its findings: https://oracy.inparliament.uk/
- Oracy Cambridge is a starting point for understanding the case for oracy and some of the available resources for teachers: https://oracycambridge.org/

2 Putting classroom talk into practice

Chapter preview

The previous chapter made the argument for the place of talk in classrooms. This chapter provides some examples of what is already known about how principles have been put into practice and signposts some starting points and resources that may be useful. It also considers school-level motivations, potential challenges and useful common criteria or reference points. The chapter covers:

- Different perspectives on classroom talk
- Understanding the evidence base for classroom talk
- Exploring schools' motivations: the impetus for change
- Acknowledging perceived challenges associated with talk
- Establishing common reference points for talk

Different perspectives on classroom talk

Before looking into the ways that schools have got started with their own journeys, it is important to consider the existing knowledge base in this field. What is the current understanding of the role of talk in learning? How do we know about this and what remains uncertain? To begin with, it should be acknowledged that exploring talk can take many forms. Summaries of a long line of research[1] reflect a wide variety of perspectives, building on those basic questions about *purpose, form and participation* – the why, how and who of talk – raised in Chapter 1. Let's begin with this example from a secondary mathematics classroom.

Classroom example: finding the perimeter

James hands out sets of cards to his Year 7 mathematics students at Brookfield. The cards each ask a question about highest common factors or lowest common multiples, a topic that students have previously spent some time working on. 'I want you to cut out each card and then, with your partner, to sort them all into three groups, gold, silver and bronze, according to how challenging you think they might be to solve,' he says.

As students sort their cards, they debate with their partners which group is most appropriate for each problem. After a few minutes, James draws the class together to consider examples of each level of potential difficulty. 'What influenced your decision-making?' he asks. Students from around the room offer a range of different reasons for regarding certain questions as being easier to answer. Some draw attention to pairs of numbers in the same multiplication table; others make a case for easy multiples and some argue simply for smaller numbers being easiest. Accepting all of these as valid perspectives, James then asks, 'Does the group you've put a question in affect how you will go about working on it?' More group discussion, supported by jotting on mini whiteboards, follows as students consider together which questions require more extended working out using techniques such as factor trees and which can be answered with more straightforward mental strategies.

How could we begin to make sense of the role of spoken language in this episode? The variety of research traditions in this field suggests that, depending on our perspective, we might be interested in, for example:

- *Establishing in a systematic way how frequently different talk types and speakers feature in a learning episode*: In James's lesson, students' talk is sometimes directed to a partner, sometimes to the wider group and sometimes to the teacher. What is the proportion of each?
- *Describing in linguistic terms the structure and function of spoken interactions*: As James asks the students to explain their decision-making, what are the patterns of interaction in terms of initiation and different forms of response?
- *Measuring the impact of implementing talk-based strategies on 'external' criteria, such as attainment*: If James has chosen to value dialogue and informal reasoning as well as direct instruction, what is the likely impact on attainment for these students?
- *Analysing and making sense of the role of spoken language as a tool for learning and an object of learning within specific contexts*: As these Year 7 students talk to one another, are they creating productive dialogue involving co-constructing ideas, or a series of disjointed contributions?

- *Exploring educators' experiences of implementing talk-based strategies*: Why has James moved away from a predominantly teacher-led lesson towards valuing diverse contributions from students? How confident does he feel in doing so?

The way that research studies have been conducted also varies considerably along different dimensions. For example, some take the form of small-scale, in-depth analyses of talk episodes, while others are larger-scale quantitative studies. Some focus on interaction in small groups, while others are geared towards whole-class or even whole-school processes. Some seek to understand and categorize the *status quo*, while others evaluate the impact of interventions. When this body of research is taken as a whole, it is clear that it is skewed in certain directions. Most of the work is distinctly Western, with the vast majority emerging from the US and UK; English, mathematics and science are over-represented as subject areas; much of the work has come from primary and lower secondary classrooms (particularly ages 8 to 14); small-scale qualitative research dominates and there are relatively few large-scale trials providing robust evidence of impact on attainment.

Understanding the evidence base for classroom talk

Examples of evidence-informed insights

As one starting point, the Education Endowment Foundation's 'Teaching and Learning Toolkit'[2] offers a meta-analysis of what it terms 'oral language interventions'. These interventions, which include strategies such as extending vocabulary, using structured questioning and promoting purposeful dialogue, are judged to have 'very high impact [on attainment] for very low cost based on extensive evidence.' As noted already, there are questions to be asked about a 'what works' view and indeed the very feasibility of meaningfully analysing disparate studies in this way. Nevertheless, such resources can help teachers to decide what actions might most profitably warrant their time, attention and effort. From this perspective, there are various talk-based practices that are well researched and potentially powerful if enacted well. By way of illustration, here are just three examples of insights for everyday practice which are strongly grounded in research. The underlying principles will be revisited in Chapters 4, 5 and 6 respectively.

1 The longstanding domination of classroom interaction by a narrow, three-part initiation, response, feedback (IRF) structure can be limiting for students. A particularly good focus of attention is the third, feedback, move. Closing off the thinking prematurely can be avoided by, for example, asking further questions or soliciting more student responses. Strategies such as querying and requesting elaboration of ideas are likely to lead to enhanced responses that make the thinking more visible.[3]
2 Talk among students can sometimes lack purpose and cohesion. Productive forms of peer talk depend on setting up the conditions for collaboration and

the task itself in structured ways. Alongside group composition, one factor is the choice of task itself. Tasks 'engineered' to require the consideration of different perspectives and that are sufficiently open-ended and challenging are likely to yield better talk outcomes.[4] Another prerequisite is the explicit teaching of *how* to collaborate, through joint agreement, and perhaps modelling, of ground rules.[5]

3 Dialogic teaching, as set out by Alexander, involves a commitment to valuing and exploring diverse perspectives and providing more student ownership of learning. While this is often challenging for teachers to realize fully, a more achievable first goal is creating a learning environment that is collective, reciprocal and supportive.[6] Establishing this overarching ethos, which allows a broad repertoire of talk types, might begin, for example, with a greater emphasis on *listening* as a skill.

These existing insights help to inform but also to understand practice by directing our attention to certain issues. Consider the following brief classroom episode.

Classroom example: peer talk as lesson opener

As students file into Fairway's Year 6 classroom after break time, Nicola is at the door, prompting them to grab mini whiteboards and get talking. It is clear that this is a familiar opening routine. The mathematics prompt displayed today concerns fractions. The class has previously learned about comparing fractions and up for discussion now are a number of statements about indicators of fraction sizes. They include some that are ambiguous and some that represent common misconceptions. As pairs of students talk and consider each statement, they use their whiteboards to sketch examples to help test or substantiate their arguments.

After 5 minutes or so, Nicola stops the class. 'Interesting,' she says, 'I've heard very different opinions on tables around the room. Before we hear some of them, what language might we need if we are going to disagree?' In response, students indicate speech bubbles on the wall showing sentence structures and specifically the one labelled 'To challenge'. Based on her discussion with a group moments before, and speaking from a position at the back of the classroom, Nicola begins by inviting Asim to go to the front and share his and his partner's thinking with the visualizer, using the rough sketches of bar models on his board. When Asim has finished making his case, Nicola opens the idea to the rest of the class: 'Can anyone build on that? Can you add to that?'

Making connections with the three insights above, we might, for example, notice that Nicola's lesson:

1 though based on more directly taught prior knowledge, has today moved beyond three-part, teacher-initiated questioning to seek a cumulative chain of student responses to an initial stimulus;

2 begins with a paired task that has a built-in need for discussion about different perspectives and uses whiteboards and discussion guidance to ensure the task remains purposeful;

3 allows the teacher to step back physically and metaphorically from the front to take a genuine interest in students' ideas, as they learn from one another and collectively build understanding in a supportive, respectful environment.

Each research-informed insight might also potentially help Nicola to develop her practice further, of course, and teacher-oriented online resources are increasingly available to support teachers in this endeavour. Voice 21,[7] Oracy Cambridge[8] and The University of Pittsburgh's Institute for Learning[9] are prominent sources of such materials. Their output includes evidence-informed programmes and products which distil principles of productive classroom talk into accessible guidance and resources for teachers. In the chapters to follow, a number of these programmes (and associated links) will be mentioned, including: Thinking Together,[10] Accountable Talk,[11] Philosophy for Children[12] and Reciprocal Teaching.[13]

By now, it should be clear that there are many justifications for a focus on classroom talk and that there is a considerable body of existing evidence and implementation guidance available. Building on the general arguments for talk from Chapter 1, let's now consider more specifically the immediate motivations for change at school level.

Exploring schools' motivations: the impetus for change

In the UK, talk in schools has had a chequered history in policy terms. Its importance across curriculum subjects has been highlighted in influential reports such as the 1975 Bullock Report[14] and acknowledged, albeit in a limited way, within English curricula in guises such as Speaking and Listening and Spoken Language.[15] Projects aimed at developing teacher expertise, such as Language in the National Curriculum and the National Oracy Project[16] from more than three decades ago, produced valuable teacher-oriented materials but their school-level influence was short-lived. Significantly for this book's attempt to adopt a broad definition of classroom talk, it has been suggested that such initiatives have fallen foul of successive governments' orientations towards two important issues which will be explored in the chapters to follow. The first is a perceived need to uphold standard English and the other is a deep-rooted scepticism about anything seen to promote 'unproductive' peer talk and collaboration.[17]

In 2021, the Speak for Change report from the Oracy APPG Inquiry once again brought spoken language back to the fore.[18] In an echo of the arguments put forward in Chapter 1, the case was made for oracy in cognitive, social and aspirational terms with a particular focus on disadvantaged groups. Three key conclusions were that oracy needs to have a higher status, be based on shared expectations and that teachers should be supported and empowered to implement strategies across all age phases and curriculum subjects. While covering the full spectrum of issues, the inquiry placed strong emphasis on spoken language as a life skill and issue of equity, perhaps making this latest incarnation of oracy more politically palatable.

Turning to the schools featured in this book, many of these arguments are reflected in their own motivations for change, which were generally aligned with one or more of the following, sometimes overlapping, beliefs.

School examples: motivations for getting started

1 Improving spoken language is the key to unlocking higher attainment across a school.
   'We'd always had this glass ceiling of attainment and we were banging and banging and not really getting those outcomes that we so desperately wanted, in spite of having great teachers and great things going on in the school ... We really know our school and community, but we were looking for that thing that was missing.' (Woodham)
2 Students need a wider range of attributes, beyond academic attainment, for life beyond school.
   'In terms of outcomes, we'd never really had an issue, but part of the vision and mission was looking at not only educational excellence and safety and wellbeing, but also preparing students for adult life. We felt when some students left us ... making that transition is quite difficult for a lot of our students. Them being able to harness their voice ... we really felt there was a gap there.' (Fairway)
3 Spoken language can close an opportunity and equity gap for some groups of students (see Box 4).
   'We were finding this massive gap for our deprived students: the ones who don't get to talk at home and who don't understand language. That was a major issue and we wanted to do something across the whole school.' (Riverside)
4 Children have the right to be heard as agents of change.
   'It's the absolute commitment to the rights of the child, UNICEF, children being agents of change – advocacy and agency are really at the core of what we do. It's a very diverse community and we wanted children to have a voice. It's very important, the right to be heard. (Underwood)

In these starting points are echoes of the arguments for talk, based on cognitive benefits (quotation 1), communicative competence (quotations 2 and 3) and participation (quotation 4). Common to all is a belief that high-quality spoken language is associated with gains for students.

Box 4

Research in focus: early language and wellbeing

The Early Intervention Foundation (EIF) is a charity researching and promoting the use of early interventions to improve the lives of children. As part of this mission, a comprehensive summary of international research on language and its links to wellbeing was undertaken.[19]

The research found social and economic disadvantage strongly linked to later outcomes for children. As well as lower academic attainment, a range of other, overlapping outcomes are associated with this starting point, including issues with behaviour, mental health and the criminal justice system. The factors at play are complex and intersecting but it is notable that language skills on entry to school are a particularly strong predictor of later academic success and that learning gaps will tend to increase during the school years.

While there is a danger of adopting a purely deficit view (see the work in Chapter 3 on assets from families) it is important to remember in any case that these societal starting points do not *determine* later outcomes; they are amenable to change. Significantly, when the home environment is examined more closely, it is specifically the lack of exposure to varied language use – not just vocabulary but *forms of interaction* – in some families which appears to have the most impact.

Two other insights from the EIF seem especially relevant for classroom practitioners:

1 While basic speech development early in life is largely a natural and resilient process, language difficulties go beyond basic talk to the complex 'pragmatic' aspects of both conveying and interpreting ideas within a range of contexts.
2 There is a need for greater coherence in professional training and vocabulary if a better shared understanding of language needs is to be established.

The EIF's report therefore underlines the case for the continued *explicit and structured* teaching of spoken language throughout schooling. Crucially, however, this teaching should concern not just surface-level communication but the place of speaking and listening in skilled interaction and as a tool for wider learning.

Acknowledging the perceived challenges

Despite the strong evidence base for classroom talk and a wealth of resources, the fact remains that developing talk is perceived as a challenge by some teachers. Millard and Menzies[20] surveyed over 900 UK teachers as part of an attempt to understand 'the state of speaking' in schools. Alongside strong support for the principle of oracy, teachers' concerns included:

- perceptions of a lack of time

- low student confidence in speaking
- student behaviour
- schools' prioritization of written work
- their own confidence in the classroom
- relevance to all subjects
- school leaders' buy-in.

Much of this is echoed in a summary of research relating to classroom dialogue more specifically by Snell and Lefstein[21] who also identify: a crowded curriculum with high-stakes tests; the need to relinquish a degree of control and demands on teachers' subject knowledge. Significantly, these authors also question teachers' low expectations of some learners, based on their attainment history, which raises the broader issue of inclusive talk practices. Some of these concerns were echoed by the schools featured in this book and five broad themes are discernible.

School examples: implementation challenges

1 What if the lesson goes in a direction I'm not prepared for?
   'There is very much that feeling of a loss of control where all this is going on around you and you're like a rabbit in the headlights. You can still have a plan but it's just how prepared you are to deviate and digress. There might be fantastic teachable moments but newer teachers don't feel comfortable with it.' (Brookfield)
2 How do I cover all this curriculum content?
   'There's often a real culture of accountability. In some subjects, you have content worries. There's so much content to cover, so a lot of the "why" is around what's the benefit here and how is this making the content stick?' (Fairway)
3 What if there's no evidence in my books to show progress?
   'It was a bit of a leap of faith at the beginning. We bought into the evidence from Cambridge or wherever but, in our context, was this going to lead to a huge drop in SATs results and our books looking really bad? That was our risk.' (Downland)
4 Why would I swap a highly functioning, quiet classroom for lots of noise?
   'It's the age-old thing of walking into a noisy classroom and it looking like chaos. There's that fear of, if the head teacher walks past, I want them to see all the students working in silence. It's almost jumping out of your comfort zone and losing control. You know if you're being observed and you do hands up, it's safer and you can control that.' (Riverside)
5 What about the reluctant speakers or quieter students?
   'Not everybody's a talker. They do not want to, and I'll be honest with you, I was one of those children when I was young. I wasn't confident enough to speak in front of everybody.' (Rushton)

So, despite strong motivations for promoting talk, there are some very reasonable questions about implementation. Some of these can be illustrated and partially addressed through the following excerpt from a Year 9 history lesson.

School example: acknowledging the challenge of presentational talk

At Southlea, Year 9 students have spent much of the lesson talking in small groups about the outcomes of World War Two. There has been lively debate in their small groups and a good level of reasoning, based on evidence, as competing views were explored. Now their teacher wants to shift to an episode based on a different form of talk. 'I want you to try and sum up your thinking by writing a perfect speech to share with others,' says Isobel. 'You can draw on all the resources and evidence you have been using.' The time allocated for drafting and the prospect of sharing beyond the immediate table group mean that this will be a more presentational form of talk than the preceding discussions and there are sentence stems on the board as prompts. However, this preparation is just a 5-minute task and involves only informal notes, rather than polished pieces of writing in books. Written work will follow in a subsequent lesson.

'Is there anyone who would like the opportunity to share?' asks Isobel when the 5 minutes is up. A list of volunteers is noted, guidelines for being a good listener are reiterated and students are invited to 'use the classroom as you choose' by opting to sit or stand as they present. As each student shares their brief summary, peers offer specific points of constructive feedback and the speaker is then asked to nominate the next person. After the first few contributions, it is the turn of Emily. Emily has agreed to her name being on the list but is now reluctant to speak out in front of the class. Rather than forcing the issue or simply moving on, Isobel gently probes for the reasons behind this reticence, suggesting that this is something everyone can learn from. With encouragement, Emily explains to the class that she is not particularly nervous about speaking in front of others in general, but hates doing this in lessons when 'everyone is staring at me and judging'. Isobel asks the other students how they feel about this and a brief discussion about the challenges and feelings associated with public speaking ensues. Although this group has already had an oral assessment in history this year, Isobel reassures them that next term they will study speech techniques in more detail so it is something they will continue to work on. Eventually, Emily feels able to share ideas with the class in a limited way.

Building in these talk-based outcomes, including formal presentations, across the curriculum is something that Southlea is committed to, but this is not without its challenges, as the above episode illustrates. The school's oracy lead explains that 'so many of our students have so little confidence' and the expectation of presenting in front of the class had initially led to claims of anxiety, communications from parents and requests from form tutors for exemptions. While the school has held firm on this expectation, it has become clear, therefore, that this needs to be acknowledged through a gradual, supported process: 'So we found we needed that really explicit teaching of the physical aspects and getting the students to present as many times as possible, even in small groups, before they do the big [assessment] points.'

Considering firstly the question of curriculum coverage, we can see that this episode has a clear place and role in a sequence of learning. The preceding group discussions have been based on substantive content in the form of historical evidence and this more open, 'exploratory' discussion has been used as a stepping stone towards a more polished – and now well-informed – presentational use of talk. This in turn will later feed into some written work. Despite the initial open debate, considerable structure remains and Isobel retains a degree of control of the overall subject matter. This valuable talking phase is given added legitimacy by the fact that oral assessment has been built into units of work. The emphasis on ground rules for speaking and listening and the breaking of the lesson time into brief talking episodes help Isobel to keep learning purposeful and on task. When it comes to speaking more publicly, sentence stems are among the structures available to help students organize their ideas. The issue of reluctance is handled sensitively: while maintaining an expectation of participation, nervousness is acknowledged and discussed as a teaching point in its own right.

Establishing common reference points for talk

Repertoires for talk

It will be clear from the preceding sections that, as well as some understanding of current insights into talk, a sense of vision and purpose is needed if these ideas are to be put into practice. The third piece of the foundational jigsaw proposed here is an understanding of models of talk that can be used as reference points for practice.

Perhaps the best known and extensive typology of talk has been developed over the last two decades by Robin Alexander,[22] largely initiated by the international research described in Box 5.

Box 5

Research in focus: the 'five cultures' study

In 2000, Robin Alexander published the outcomes of a large-scale and seminal research project.[23] The 'five cultures' study is a comparison of primary education across schools in Russia, India, France, the USA and England. The commentary zooms in progressively from national policy and curricula to school environments and routines and finally to lesson structures and specific instances of interaction. By the end of the extensive analysis, Alexander identifies the empowerment of students as a central theme and, significantly, singles out approaches to the pedagogy of spoken language as the most important outcome of the comparative analysis.

From his starting point as an English educator, it is often to Russia that Alexander turns for the most intriguing contrasts. The many insights into differences in learning discourse from the close scrutiny of classroom transcripts include the following three interrelated points, which may provoke thought about accepted practices in your own classroom:

1 English and particularly North American classrooms prize the affective aspects of talk, with opportunities to share and collaborate valued as ends in their own right. In contrast to this emphasis on *learning to talk*, students in the other countries *talk to learn* to a greater extent, with a less negotiated, less democratic and more teacher-directed, structured form of discourse.

2 Russian and Indian classroom discourse tends to feature a more formal 'subject' register with an expectation of students employing more specific terminology and articulating ideas precisely. This register, in contrast to the more 'vernacular' conversational forms seen in the USA and England, may allow for the more effective development of shared understanding.

3 Unlike in England and the USA, where the teacher's aim is often a brief exchange with as many students as possible, whole-class episodes in Russia, in particular, tend to see engagement with fewer respondents but for a prolonged sequence of more in-depth questions. In line with the superiority of the class as a collective entity over the individual, Russian students are thought of as answering on behalf of their peers whose participation takes the form of careful watching and listening.

To a great extent, these differing norms, relating to purpose, form and participation respectively, reflect wider national orientations and values. Rather than seeing one form of discourse as inherently better than another, Alexander's international comparisons help us to question taken-for-granted assumptions and draw attention to the fact that in countries such as Russia, spoken language has a high status in the classroom and is therefore a carefully considered part of everyday interactions.

Alexander proposes categories of learning talk as just one of a number of 'repertoires' for teachers, which represent talk in terms of settings, forms and specific moves. Recognizing that no form of talk is inherently good or bad, his work emphasizes above all the exercise of teachers' judgement on fitness for purpose, rather than adherence to a particular approach. The broad range of learning talk therefore comprises the following functions, which might each take a number of forms:

- transactional: manage encounters and situations
- expository: narrate, expound and explain

- interrogatory: ask questions
- exploratory: venture, explore and probe ideas
- deliberative: reason and argue
- imaginative: contemplate and articulate what might be
- expressive: articulate thoughts, ideas and feelings
- evaluative: articulate opinions and judgements.

Although the focus of this book is chiefly on students' talk, Alexander's separate categorization of teacher-initiated talk is also of interest, since it is this which will typically begin any interaction. While firmly acknowledging the value and place of teacher-led, instructional modes such as rote, recitation, instruction and exposition, Alexander notes that there is a further group of talk types that are less common but likely to be more generative of high-quality student talk:

- discussion: exchanging ideas and information
- deliberation: weighing the merits of ideas, opinions or evidence
- argumentation: making or testing a case through reasoning and use of evidence
- dialogue: working towards a collective understanding in an interactive way.

The characteristics of dialogue will be covered in Chapter 6 but it is clear that without these four stances on the part of the teacher, the full range of opportunities for students is unlikely to be offered.

A framework for talk

Unlike this focus on the varied *purposes* of talk, the Oracy Framework in Figure 2 provides a breakdown of the *skills* that form the building blocks of talk across a range of purposes.[24] The Framework was developed by the University of Cambridge and Voice 21 as part of a broader project to develop an assessment toolkit for oracy. While approaches to, and even the desirability of, assessing oracy remain the subject of debate and will be explored further in Chapter 8, the Framework component of this project has become a prominent reference point for schools across age phases.[25]

The Oracy Framework sets out to specify the observable features of effective talk that can apply to any talk situation in a range of classroom contexts. It breaks down oracy into four broad categories of skill:

1 Physical
2 Linguistic
3 Cognitive
4 Social and emotional.

A quick glance at these four areas (broken into fourteen sub-categories) shows that this is a fairly comprehensive, holistic view of spoken language

Figure 2 The Oracy Framework

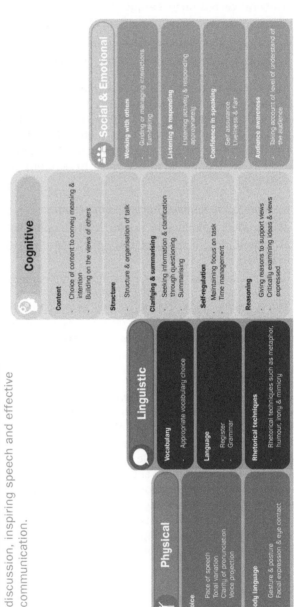

The Oracy Framework

Use the oracy framework to understand the physical, linguistic, cognitive, and social and emotional skills that enable successful discussion, inspiring speech and effective communication.

Oracy
Cambridge

Physical

Voice
- Pace of speech
- Tonal variation
- Clarity of pronunciation
- Voice projection

Body language
- Gesture & posture
- Facial expression & eye contact

Linguistic

Vocabulary
- Appropriate vocabulary choice

Language
- Register
- Grammar

Rhetorical techniques
- Rhetorical techniques such as metaphor, humour, irony & mimicry

Cognitive

Content
- Choice of content to convey meaning & intention
- Building on the views of others

Structure
- Structure & organisation of talk

Clarifying & summarising
- Seeking information & clarification through questioning
- Summarising

Self-regulation
- Maintaining focus on task
- Time management

Reasoning
- Giving reasons to support views
- Critically examining ideas & views expressed

Social & Emotional

Working with others
- Guiding or managing interactions
- Turn-taking

Listening & responding
- Listening actively & responding appropriately

Confidence in speaking
- Self assurance
- Liveliness & flair

Audience awareness
- Taking account of level of understand of the audience

voice 21

© Voice 21, 2020 developed in partnership with Oracy Cambridge. Voice 21 is a registered charity in England and Wales. Charity number 1155321 | Company no. 09145795

skills, covering the functional building blocks of talk. While a focus *wholly* on skills and communicative competence would risk being potentially reductive,[26] this framework provides a user-friendly shared object for students and teachers alike and is a valuable starting point. Building on the Framework, Voice 21 has also developed a set of benchmarks[27] to exemplify these principles in practice at both teacher and whole-school levels and to serve as a self-evaluation tool. For individual teachers, the five aspirational descriptors, mirrored by comparable aims at whole-school level, include valuing every voice, teaching oracy explicitly and harnessing oracy to elevate learning. In these materials, there is a hint of some of the important issues to be explored in subsequent chapters, particularly the high status accorded to talk as both an object of learning and a pedagogical tool and a commitment to student participation and progress in this venture. Structures such as the Oracy Framework potentially offer a common language and set of values, therefore, but school-level ownership and identity remain important, as seen in the following example.

School example: taking ownership

The four strands of the Oracy Framework, referred to as the 'fundamentals' underpin Riverside's oracy provision in three major ways. Firstly, a concept map outlines and defines five types of activity that will support this skill development across the school: reasoning, discussion, listening, debate and speech. This provides a common understanding and language for staff and students alike. These fundamental skills from the Framework then also inform a discrete oracy curriculum for each year group, closely linked to PSHE, which is enacted during tutor time and reinforced through extra-curricular activity. Finally, a progression document has been created. This identifies facets of each strand ('small wins that they build up as they go along') and particular challenges, which can be targeted each year and self-assessed by students. Rather than simply ticking off each target, students are required to explain to staff how they have achieved them. The oracy lead recounts one example:

'I've got a Year 10 tutor group and one of them came up to me and said "Miss, guess what? I answered for the first time in class today. I shared an answer." So they're speaking to us to explain it. But if you knew anything about that child, they don't normally talk, so it's little things like that – trying to get them excited for it.'

Riverside's example illustrates how one school takes ownership of external resources in line with its own priorities. Chapter 3 will consider how structures such as this are used in practice to teach students how to use spoken language.

Questions for reflection

- What groundwork is needed to ensure that students are ready to develop their spoken language in terms of behaviour and confidence to speak?
- How might you reconcile the pressures of curriculum coverage, evidence of learning and attainment with more opportunities for talk?
- How might you ensure that talk opportunities are accessible to all and that all learners participate?

Related resources

- Voice 21's website has a huge range of teacher resources and features The Oracy Framework and Oracy Benchmarks mentioned in this chapter: https://voice21.org/
- Robin Alexander's website has a range of readings and resources: https://robinalexander.org.uk/dialogic-teaching/
- The Speech, Language and Communication Framework is a self-evaluation tool developed by the Communication Trust: https://www.slcframework.org.uk/the-speech-language-and-communication-framework-slcf/

3 | Learning to talk and listen

Chapter preview

Building on the starting points outlined in Chapter 2, this chapter begins to explore how such a focus might be enacted in practice. In reality, of course, learning *to* talk and learning *through* talk are intertwined and mutually enhancing. However, this chapter focuses on the former through a consideration of both how the foundations for learning through talk might be laid and how developing spoken language can also be viewed as a legitimate end in itself. The chapter covers:

- Insights to frame the practice
- Creating opportunities for talk
- Structures: scaffolding talk
- Talking about talk: the metacognitive dimension
- A skill for life and the question of standard English
- Conversations: listening as well as speaking

Insights to frame the practice

There is a persuasive case for schools focusing on the effective use of spoken language as a learning goal in its own right (as opposed to as a pedagogical tool for other learning). Good oral communication is prized by employers[1] and is related to peer social acceptance in young children;[2] conversely, early Speech, Language and Communication Needs (SLCN) are strongly related to lower educational outcomes and are also predictors of wider future challenges involving employment, mental health and the criminal justice system.[3] SLCN are much more prevalent for children from lower socioeconomic backgrounds,[4] providing a strong social justice argument for this form of teaching too. Nevertheless, questions arise about what constitutes effective language use and its place in the curriculum and wider work of schools.

As noted in Chapter 1, spoken language learning in schools is frequently associated with the work of Andrew Wilkinson.[5] He coined the term 'oracy' in the 1960s to argue for it having high status alongside other fundamental skills such as literacy. Since then, the term has sometimes been used as a broad, catch-all term for spoken language in the classroom. Neil Mercer[6] makes a distinction between the explicit teaching of speaking and listening skills and teaching approaches using spoken language. Robin Alexander[7] makes a similar distinction between developmental and pedagogical aspects of talk, while stressing their close connection. Unpicking oracy as a concept in this way is important, as oral pedagogies (related to learning through talk) have connotations with teaching strategies that fall in and out of favour at policy and school level. On the other hand, an emphasis on speaking and listening skills – more related to the idea of 'communicative competence'[8] – presupposes no specific pedagogical stance and may be less contentious in this respect.

When teaching students how to talk effectively, schools use a wide range of strategies such as establishing varied opportunities for speaking, introducing vocabulary, modelling by teachers, providing sentence structures and explicitly evaluating spoken language.[9] There are some important caveats, however. Firstly, research from early childhood suggests that it is not sheer exposure to spoken language, or vocabulary, that is the biggest predictor of later academic success, but rather the nature of that exposure and, more specifically, involvement in *conversational turn-taking* from a young age.[10] There is also the question of what counts as high-quality language. The richness and fluency of children's spoken language in diverse home environments and cultures are not always valued in the school setting[11] and concerns have been raised about the wider implications for inclusion, participation and teacher expectations of imposing 'correct' or 'standard' language.[12] As part of an attempt to provide a basis for spoken language assessment, Mercer[13] and colleagues from academic and school settings created and refined the Oracy Framework introduced in Chapter 2. While its evaluation as part of an assessment toolkit focused on lower secondary students, the framework more generally provides a shared understanding, terminology and object of focus that can be used by teachers and students alike.

As we explore some of the examples from classrooms, pertinent questions to keep in mind include the following:

• The extent to which it is possible, or desirable, to separate the teaching of spoken language skills from oral pedagogies.
• How teachers move beyond use of vocabulary and sentence structures to focus also on communicative competence more broadly.
• The ways in which some form of common framework and terminology may help teachers and students to consider spoken language at a metacognitive level.
• How a balance is struck between 'correct' forms of language and the valuing of students' dialects.

Creating opportunities for talk

One starting point for children learning to use spoken language is to ensure that they inhabit an everyday environment that is rich in high-quality talk.

Opportunities to talk in classrooms need to encompass a range that includes formal, 'presentational' modes of speech, imaginative or creative uses of language and the often-messy use of what Graham Nuthall called 'private peer talk,'[14] or talk as a tool for thinking. What these diverse modes have in common is their potential for teachable moments through which students are helped to improve their communication in each register. The schools featured in this book offer a wide variety of opportunities, from exploratory talk in lessons in which no written work is expected to platforms for public performance in poetry slams, persuasive speeches to the school community and inter-class debates.

The two contrasting examples from primary schools which follow illustrate the power of clarity around the context, purpose and audience for speaking and listening,[15] one generating fairly spontaneous talk and the other very formal.

Classroom example: a language-rich environment

In Queensway's Reception classroom, a small group has just been enjoying the story of The Little Red Hen. Christine invites children to choose puppets representing each character and then leads a joint re-telling using a pictorial story map. Individual characters join in with key lines at appropriate moments. After this very structured and relatively formal use of talk, attention turns to the role play area. This has been set up with objects to bring the story to life: pictures of wheat growing in the field and farm animals adorn the walls, while two tables are stocked with eggs, milk, flour and baking equipment. The children are invited to act out the story and Christine's role shifts to facilitating the talk to accompany the actions. Sometimes the talk is with her ('So what happens next?') and sometimes between peers ('Come and tell him what you're doing. I'm not sure he heard').

This sort of open, imaginative role play as a stimulus for talk is common in the early years but encountered much less often with older children. At Queensway, however, students all the way up to 11 years old take part in an 'Aspirations Week' of themed work in which classrooms are transformed into workplace settings such as an airport, a garden centre, a vet's practice and even a wellness spa. Working in mixed age groups, older students' participation is legitimized and encouraged through 'helping' the younger children. Students visit these varied settings and engage in imaginative talk based on topic prompts, sentence stems and target vocabulary that is made available. Talk is heavily modelled by teachers and the range of forms includes reporting on events at the media centre and even politely, but assertively, complaining about the food at the in-house restaurant!

Classroom example: the courtroom

'Court ended!' The judge at the front of the hall bangs his gavel and brings proceedings to a close. It is the conclusion of a heated Year 5 'trial' at Rushton Primary. In the dock has been the proposal that the school should have a social media account. Prosecution and defence lawyers, rising from their separate tables in front of the judge, have made well-reasoned cases, sporadically interrupting their opponents with passionate objections. Following the summing-up ('Ladies and gentlemen of the jury ...'), the jurors seated to the side of the courtroom have offered up individual thoughts to their peers.

The process is choreographed throughout by Anji, the teacher, offering prompts not on content but on presentation ('Use a nice clear voice'; 'Face the jurors'). In this scenario, arguments and key speeches have been researched and pre-prepared, leaving space for a clear focus on the physical aspects of talk geared to engaging with an audience, such as projection, posture and eye contact. As Anji says afterwards:

They understood it all and had all the evidence, but it's the learning to talk they struggle with, coming in at the right time or having a clear voice and projecting rather than shouting. It's building on those things now.'

The juxtaposition of these two examples seems at first to represent two extremes: the informal, conversational use of language in everyday tasks contrasted with the peculiar high formality of the courtroom. However, the examples also have much in common.

In both settings, children are engaged in talk for a clear purpose: they are using language in a functional way to get something done. While these examples are presented out of context, they are of course the culmination of both thorough teacher preparation and student prior learning. In the Reception class, the students are already familiar with the book in question and the role play area has been carefully equipped to stimulate their talk. In the Year 5 trial, arguments have been drafted and rehearsed and there is a prior understanding of some idiosyncratic courtroom procedures and language (in this respect, there is much in common with the work in other schools on the conventions of formal debating). While, in both cases, specific vocabulary and phrasing are prominent, the greater focus is on the forms of interaction appropriate in that setting. Recent research suggests that we need to look beyond simply the deficit view of a 'word gap' and also address turn-taking as the more powerful early experience in terms of its provision of opportunities for both practice and feedback.[16] While this research focuses on adult-child turn-taking, some of the benefits might be achieved using other children as the 'more knowledgeable other', as seen in the mixed-age interaction during Queensway's Aspiration Week.

Christine's involvement in the first example bears some of the hallmarks of sustained shared thinking (SST). This is a form of dialogue, often involving adult modelling and open questioning, aimed at promoting shared thinking around a joint activity. While SST is associated mainly with the early years, it can be seen as part of a continuum towards dialogic teaching more broadly, as discussed in Chapter 6.[17] Indeed, the active role of the teacher during what are superficially student-led activities is another common feature of both episodes. Anji's prompts in the courtroom maintain a clear focus on the presentational aspects of talk as the main objective of this event and she also acts to stage-manage proceedings. Meanwhile, Christine's role in Reception shifts from modelling to questioning and finally to promoting peer interaction, showing the transfer of responsibility that we will explore in the next section.

Structures: scaffolding talk

Chapter 2 began to explore how schools have brought talk to the fore and made it an explicit object of learning. In doing so, it also touched on the delicate balance to be struck between guiding children towards more effective forms of oral communication and avoiding a sense of 'policing' or closing down the rich linguistic diversity heard in schools – a balance we will return to later in this chapter. A compromise frequently struck is to offer and model language structures that can be adapted for use in specific situations, sometimes in the form of sentence starters or 'stems'. As the following examples from primary and secondary contexts illustrate, these devices are powerful if used with judgement and flexibility.

Listening to learners: children using prompts and roles

A Year 5 student at Rushton describes prompts in personal diaries:
   'There's a page all about oracy with speech bubbles of sentence starters. When it's oracy time, everyone gets their books out, goes to that page and when we're having discussions, we can use that starter to talk in the discussion. Because you don't want to just say all the time "I agree" or "I disagree", there are lots of better starters you can use. It improves your talking.'

Meanwhile, at Woodham, Year 4 students describe other useful structures:
   'You get given special jobs to do sometimes in a group, which have different rules, like the builder who builds on other people and the challenger who has to challenge people's ideas and the balancer who then balances the ideas ... At the front of the class is something called the listening ladder. Whenever you need to listen to someone talk, you need to do all those things to be a good listener ... When we need to talk to our table, we put our thumb in so they know we want to talk.'

Building on these primary examples, we can see similar structures at work, in an age-appropriate way, in this secondary classroom at Southlea.

Classroom example: using sentence stems to build arguments for whole-class sharing

In Graham's Year 8 English class, pairs of students are discussing Susan Hill's *The Woman in Black*. In doing so, they use sentence stems displayed on the board such as: 'One impression created is …' and 'This highlights …' to help them articulate their views and draw upon evidence from the text. Having talked this through in pairs, specific students are invited to stand up and share their analysis using these linguistic structures.

Graham begins by reminding the rest of the class about how to be a good audience through giving eye contact and showing interest. While features of each student's initial offering to the class are noted for praise, there is also an expectation of some collective elaboration on the answer. In one case, a peer offers a subtle correction of the use of the term 'transgression' and the original contributor is invited to rephrase and develop her original response. Another student's otherwise good arguments are lacking sufficient supporting evidence from the book; suggestions are then supplied, along with page references, by someone elsewhere in the room. This sort of purposeful interaction is the result of adopting a more structured approach to talk, as Graham explains:

'In the past, when I'd had talk tasks in the classroom, it had never gone the way I wanted it to go, so I ended up stepping back from dialogic or group work as it wasn't getting the end point I wanted. It was eating into curriculum time and I was having to re-teach things later.'

Now, however, Graham approaches talk differently:

'One of the things I focused on was setting specific parameters for talk … Using things like sentence stems, key vocabulary and images on the board focuses them on what you want them to talk about. It's very clear, it shapes the discussion.'

Classroom example: modelling subject-specific terminology

At Woodham, the mathematics topic for Year 1 this week is addition and subtraction. Today, the students are seated on the carpet with individual whiteboards at the ready, working on missing number problems such as $9 + ? = 11$. As each question is collectively considered, key points are reinforced through a process of choral repetition ('Greater means bigger'; 'Add the parts and count them all') or call and response ('Remember, the whole is always the …?'; 'The biggest number').

The modelling by Rachel, their teacher, goes beyond facts and procedures, however, and extends to the wider use of sentence structures and mathematical vocabulary. She provides verbal scaffolds to help children to answer in sentences when explaining their thinking. For some, this might be in the form of a sentence starter, or stem ('It is different because ...'; 'The whole is ...') or the provision of relevant terminology, such as 'altogether' or 'part-part-whole'. For others, needing more challenge, there is a looser structure. One student is invited to: 'use the words "first", "then" and "now" to structure your answer.' In each case, when a child gives a clear answer, their response is taken as a model for the group as a whole, who are invited to repeat it chorally so that it becomes a collective response. These varied scaffolds reflect the school's commitment to offering differing levels of challenge. Over time, such structures have become internalized at this school:

'The more we've used the sentence stems and structures for talk, the more we hear it creeping into their everyday vocabulary, even in the playground!'

These examples bring to life the idea of scaffolding. Scaffolding, often associated with the work of David Wood, Jerome Bruner and colleagues, has been defined as a process that: 'enables a child or novice to solve a problem, carry out a task or achieve a goal which would be beyond his [sic] unassisted efforts.'[18] Certainly, the student testimony in the first example above illustrates a number of common forms of such assistance. However, if that were all, one might legitimately ask whether superficial eloquence is the only goal. That question is answered by the two classroom extracts which followed and which hint at the deeper learning purpose of these sentence stems and other scaffolds for speaking.

In Graham's Year 8 class, these structures ensure a focus on relevant content, but also the creation of a shared understanding of how to analyse a text. Understanding is also at the heart of Rachel's work in Year 1 as the use of specific language constructions reinforces the relationship between parts and the whole in her addition and subtraction problems. Through scaffolding the spoken language, therefore, the language in turn itself becomes a scaffold for the joint understanding of English and mathematical concepts.

Beyond the use of sentence starters and vocabulary, we also see glimpses of other forms of support as Graham coordinates peer contributions to help refine individuals' thinking and Rachel varies her levels of structure according to differing expectations of individuals. Alongside this contingent and flexible support, scaffolding is about empowerment, as explained in Box 6. In the two classrooms seen here, it is interesting to pause and speculate on how the support from the teacher and indeed peers might be gradually faded and responsibility transferred. Much of this has to do with the internalization of modelled routines and language structures or a move from 'other-regulation' to 'self-regulation'.[19] At the heart of this is the idea of metacognition, which is the subject of the next section.

Box 6

Research in focus: developing a common understanding of scaffolding

Scaffolding is a well-known idea in education, rooted in sociocultural views of learning and coined as a term by Wood, Bruner and Ross in studies of 1-1 tutoring.[20] As with many such metaphors, however, understanding and usage can vary enormously. Van de Pol and colleagues in the Netherlands undertook a systematic review of the research literature on scaffolding to try and establish a common view of what constitutes scaffolding, how it is enacted and what its effects are.[21]

Among the many definitions of scaffolding, three common features emerge consistently:

1 Contingency
2 Fading
3 Transferring responsibility.

The three are connected, since contingency (or responsive, flexible support) can eventually lead to fading of support and thereby to the gradual transfer of responsibility from teacher to student.

The review identifies six common means of scaffolding: feeding back, hinting, instructing, explaining, modelling and questioning. As part of contingency, each strategy might be varied to offer greater or lesser degrees of structure. Such activities on the part of the teacher appear to work both by reducing the student's cognitive load and through the student's internalization of the support structure so that productive strategies eventually become enacted independently.

Scaffolding can also be seen to have a variety of intentions. It has been found to have an impact on cognition (e.g. in subsequent independent task performance), metacognition (e.g. through improved reasoning and self-regulation) and, to a lesser extent, affective outcomes, such as motivation and emotion. However, the authors are also clear that the effectiveness of scaffolding is difficult to measure. This is due chiefly to a lack of reliable instruments, a need for more data collection focused on student learning rather than teacher strategies and the variability of classroom contexts. Despite the gaps in research, this review helpfully draws attention back to the essence of the scaffolding process and to the specific means and potential goals of its implementation.

Talking about talk: the metacognitive dimension

If classroom talk is to flourish, it needs to be made an explicit part of students' learning and, as such, discussed openly. The groundwork for this is in the shared terminology and frames of reference that were introduced in Chapter 2. Talking about talk links to arguments for the power of metacognition, typically described as awareness, monitoring and direction of one's thoughts and learning processes and frequently associated in research with positive out-comes for students.[22] As well as talk being a well-established tool for cultivating metacognitive strategies generally, it can also become the *object* of such attention itself.[23]

To begin with, teachers may signal that the quality of talk is valued within lessons by noticing and openly drawing attention to it. This might be in the form of teacher modelling, feedback to students or even working with a parallel set of talk-based learning objectives for each lesson. The Thinking Together website[24] includes many resources and ideas for encouraging this sort of meta-cognitive awareness. All of this serves to establish not only a high status for talk but also a powerful shared understanding for students and teachers. As seen in Chapter 1, there are many facets and purposes related to classroom talk so it is helpful to bring these together in a coherent form that allows for a common vocabulary and vision.

School example: explicit evaluation of features of talk

Jasmine, a teacher at Northside, hides her face behind a sheet of paper and almost inaudibly mumbles a series of incoherent points to her Year 8 class. Fortunately, this is not her usual teaching style, but a demonstration of how *not* to present to an audience. Her students enjoy the performance and are quick to identify and remedy all of the deficiencies.

This is a life skills lesson, an opportunity at Northside for oracy strategies to be explicitly taught and practised before they are embedded across the wider curriculum. The students are finalizing campaign presentations for various chosen causes close to their hearts. The demonstration and the students' responses allow Jasmine to make explicit and memorable the con-nections to the four strands of the Oracy Framework, which are displayed prominently on the interactive whiteboard. These strands are to provide the criteria for peer assessment of the pre-prepared presentations and, as they commence, students are reminded to be active listeners, noting specific features.

As small groups come to the front to present about issues such as home-lessness, animal testing and plastic waste, other students' feedback cen-tres on points taken from the framework. Referring to the cognitive strand, for example, persuasive language through good reasoning is highlighted, while voice projection and eye contact from the physical and vocabulary choice from the linguistic strand are also noted. Some students are under-standably nervous but Jasmine has encouragement for all: 'Come on, you can do it!'

The formal use of oracy criteria is fitting for this Year 8 class, but focused reflection on aspects of talk is equally possible for the youngest of primary students, as we can see below in Christine and Angela's classrooms.

School example: talk detectives

A large number of Year 1 and 2 children sit in groups of around five in the school hall. Wandering among them are a small band of students wearing hats adorned with ears or a magnifying glass. These are the 'talk detectives', on the hunt for good speaking and listening.

Talking in this environment as part of a large group is a new experience, so Christine, the teacher, has provided plenty of structure: children sit around large sheets of paper with numbers indicating their place; a noise meter is displayed – providing a reminder about appropriate levels of talk in this environment – and the importance of listening and reasoning are emphasized. Today's talking point is: 'Lions are scarier than dinosaurs'. This is an immediately engaging topic and students have some background knowledge to bring to the discussion. While the stimulus ensures there is plenty to say, the emphasis this time is on expressing agreement or disagreement by providing a reason. To maintain structure and focus, talk time is frequently punctuated with guidance or models of good talking overheard. As each phase of discussion concludes, Christine encourages children to stand up and share ideas publicly, with reasoning words such as 'because' singled out for attention. At the end of the session, the talk detectives are invited to the front to nominate individuals or groups who have spoken and listened particularly well, signalling that the interaction itself – as well as the content – is what is valued.

Classroom example: giving talk-specific feedback in phonics

At Eastland, Year 1 children are throwing balls of paper at targets stuck on the wall around the classroom. This is not an outbreak of rebellion, but part of today's phonics learning. Pairs of children are working together to test one another's recall of the spelling of words with a 'ph' grapheme. Today's words – already practised as a whole class – are written on slips of paper. One member of the pair selects a word to sound out and learn, through blending and segmenting its phonemes, before scrunching up the paper and throwing it at the target. The second child retrieves the paper, opens it out and asks their partner to spell the word.

Alongside learning to read and spell these words, there is a parallel oracy objective today. Across the school, students are currently focused on giving high-quality verbal feedback to their peers. The children's teacher, Angela, has modelled this from the start of the morning. As children checked in with how they were feeling, she drew attention to Ethan's response, noting specific features such as the way he had skilfully combined two thoughts with a 'First … but also …' structure. For this spelling game, Angela now models with a child some different ways of feeding back to a partner, depending on how accurate the spelling is. Some of her sentence stems, such as 'I heard you say ...' and 'The mistake you can learn from next time is ...', are displayed on the board as prompts.

Angela reminds the children that she will be noticing this aspect of their interactions: 'What I'm really looking for is the feedback. I'll be the talk detective today and I will come round and tap you if I hear you giving great feedback.' As the game proceeds and the children practise their spelling, feedback is to the fore. In one corner of the room, Maryam spells her word, dolphin, correctly. 'Good job,' says her partner. 'No,' says Maryam, 'you need to say more – tell me which bits I remembered.'

Drawing these examples together, it is immediately clear that, in different ways, talk has been given a high status in the learning. Year 8 students are asked to evaluate peers' presentations not primarily on substantive content, but on delivery. In the Year 1 and 2 example, there are students with a designated role as evaluator (indicated visually by the hat). In the final classroom, Angela explicitly signals her interest verbally ('What I'm really looking for is ...'). All of this speaks to the idea of the *hidden curriculum*. Philip Jackson[25] was among the early writers to use this term to describe the unwritten, but all-pervasive, norms influencing school learning. Much of the hidden curriculum relates to sometimes-implicit messages about what is really valued; in these examples, it is clear that talk is something worthy of attention and practice. Related to this high status is the way that these teachers – again in an age-appropriate manner – give students clear criteria for discussing the talk. Year 8 students refer to aspects of the Oracy Framework introduced in Chapter 2, while the younger children are directed, through teacher comments and sentence stems, to attend to a small number of features, such as reasoning or listening.

Box 7

Research in focus: metacognition

Although often over-simplified as 'thinking about thinking', metacognition, or the monitoring of thought processes, is a potentially complex concept. In the 1970s, developmental psychologist John Flavell proposed a new area of inquiry in learning: children's development of what he termed adult-like 'cognitive monitoring' behaviour.[26] His interest was in the interaction of metacognitive knowledge and metacognitive experiences with cognitive goals and actions.

Much more recently, the Education Endowment Foundation (EEF) position metacognition, alongside cognition and motivation, as a central component of self-regulated learning.[27] In the EEF model, metacognition involves the learner's awareness of three things:

- their own abilities
- the potential strategies available
- the nature of the task in hand.

This awareness is then applied to a cyclical process of planning, monitoring and evaluating their own response to a task. Among the EEF's recommendations are the explicit teaching of metacognitive strategies, including the teacher's modelling of their own thought processes, and the provision of an appropriate level of challenge. Especially significant for an interest in spoken language is the guidance report's recommendation to promote and develop metacognitive talk, including that between students. The specific correlation between metacognitive talk and wider attainment has been noted elsewhere.[28] Indeed, as will be seen in subsequent chapters, many of the productive talk structures linked more generally to attainment gains, such as exploratory talk (Chapter 5) and dialogic teaching (Chapter 6),[29] are inherently metacognitive in the ways that they give voice to students' ongoing understanding and thought processes.

The EEF's toolkit,[30] a meta-analysis of impact on attainment from a range of sources, suggests that metacognition is a particularly high-impact, low-cost and well-evidenced strategy for teachers, a finding supported by other recent evidence reviews.[31] With the focus of this chapter in mind, one implication for teachers is that metacognitive talk about talk itself (or 'metatalk') is likely to be very powerful.

Turning more specifically to the view of metacognition summarized in Box 7, the extracts illustrate aspects of the planning, monitoring and evaluation involved, explicitly and collectively externalized in various ways. The 'talk detective' role, for example, which will be encountered in other classrooms later in the book, relates to longstanding strategies for peer assessment through noting and reflecting on talk, as seen in the Thinking Together materials.[32] Such 'metatalk' might potentially focus on both the process and the quality of talk.[33] The intention is that these thought processes will eventually become internalized at an individual level. As well as this metacognitive focus on talk itself, these experiences provide a basis for talking about learning processes more broadly and the benefits of metacognitive talk for both formative assessment and attainment are well established in research.[34]

A further issue raised by the preceding examples is the question of where to situate this metacognitive focus on talk. Is it best developed within the context of the curriculum or handled discretely? While at Eastland this discussion was embedded in some phonics teaching, the other two extracts were from lessons set up specifically to focus on talk. Related to this, it is important to avoid the scaffolds discussed so far becoming tokenistic and decontextualized. The schools in this book approached this dilemma in a number of ways and, to return to our emphasis on professional judgement, there is no correct response. The following illustrates how one school rationalizes their approach.

> **School example: embedding talk routines**
>
> Students in Years 7 to 9 at Fairway participate in a series of one-hour Voice lessons. These lessons allow for the dedicated teaching of components of talk such as sentence structures, group roles, listening skills and balanced arguments, ready to be embedded across the curriculum. A school leader explains that ways of talking publicly are initially introduced in a discrete and explicit way:
>
> *'We teach it like a language through choral repetition and games. We say to them, "This is going to feel really awkward and clunky at first and you're going to feel really odd at first but we say the more you do it, the more you say it, the more you hear it, the more it's going to be natural. So just break through that barrier because this is a safe place to practise." We've found that very quickly students adapt to it.'*
>
> Nevertheless, there is also a recognition that merely adopting terminology can lead to an empty, superficial form of rhetoric. The need to address the cognitive elements of talk is shared openly with the students:
>
> *'That's been a big learning curve for me, making time for both exploratory talk and presentational talk. It's about having that openness with the students. Sometimes I have to say, "OK, you've got these sentence stems and it's great to hear you using them when you feed back to the whole class, but now for 5 minutes I just need you to have a chat. It's fine, I don't speak like that all the time so just be relaxed because this is about generating ideas now and working out what your opinion is." If they feel you're too hung up on formal speech and being articulate you squash their ideas, effectively. It's getting that balance. We're flexible: when we realize that the sentence stems are being picked up quickly but there's a lack of exploratory talk or confidence in developing opinion through messy talk, we're putting the emphasis there, where it's needed and we'll come back to the stems. It's not tokenistic or like a tick list where we can say they've all got that, let's move on.'*

We see here an approach involving some discrete oracy teaching, but with a view to these skills being embedded elsewhere. The question of formality and use of prescribed structures relies on a teacher's judgement about the context and it is to this issue the chapter now turns.

A skill for life and the question of standard English

In Chapters 1 and 2 the argument was made for spoken language as a skill for employability and life prospects. Indeed, the 2021 Oracy APPG report makes much of the teaching of talk having most impact on disadvantaged students, partly as a means to social mobility.[35] Certainly, secondary students at Northside perceive the potential for personal transformation.

Listening to learners: developing skills for life

There's a buzz of excitement as students articulate the benefits of working on oracy. For some, the transformation has involved building personal confidence:

'I'm shy and I don't like the big stage but, after oracy, I learned this new skill and I love to use it. Some of you might remember how I was before. I was really quiet and I never wanted to speak, but now I'm a completely different person.'

'I'm a lot more confident in speaking out. Normally, I was the person at the back, hoping I wouldn't get picked but now I'm the person who wants to get picked if I've got a good idea.'

For others, there is a recognition of the value of spoken language as a life skill:

'It gives you the skills needed for when you go to college or university and in any job you'll always have some sort of oracy, whether it's just talking to your colleagues or you're actually doing a lecture. It just really prepares you.'

'I think it disciplines and matures a person so that, when they speak, they're very calm and very eloquent. When you look at speakers, the way they speak and they interact, it's very formal and very professional. It gives a very good sense of that person. That's how you build up a reputation and that's how you'll get jobs and interviews.'

The reference in the final quotation to eloquence, formality and reputation recalls the cultural capital argument from Chapter 1 and suggests that there is an accepted, agreed standard of professional language. From a teacher's perspective, too, the use of 'correct' language for these purposes can also be an ambition. The following examples show teachers who are mindful of their students' status as, respectively, bilingual learners and future employees.

School example: modelling language for bilingual learners

Many students at Rushton have limited exposure to English in everyday life at home and this is at the forefront of teachers' minds, as one explains:

'In the classroom, we tend to want them to use more standard English because we've got EAL [English as an Additional Language] children who are learning from the others. It's modelling as much standard English as possible so that they are hearing it correctly because at home they might not, or they're hearing a home language. I wouldn't be inclined, though, to correct them if they were just with friends, on the playground, say.'

A colleague concurs:

'One of the Year 6 targets is to use language in a formal or informal style and how to differentiate between the two. Because they have EAL we're trying to teach the correct level of English and we've only got six hours a day to do it. But in paired talk in class, they'd have a very informal way of talking to their partner, which is fine. We'd encourage that because at least they are talking, as long as they're talking about the actual topic.'

At Riverside, meanwhile, teachers are eager to ensure that their students go out into the world able to compete confidently with others in interviews and employment-related situations.

School example: 'future-ready' young people

'We're trying to model as teachers how to speak and write. In my classroom, I sometimes talk as if I'm an exam answer. One issue we have is that the students speak in colloquial language even in their books. It's almost using the oracy to transfer it [from speech to writing].

One of our things is future-ready young people. It's not just about exam technique, it's understanding how to speak in different situations. Every student gets two mock interviews and there's been a massive difference in those who have had the oracy training versus those who haven't. It's confidence and self-worth as well. They don't believe they're good enough to share their voice. It sounds daft but almost by making them sound clever, everyone perks up and goes, "oh that sounds good" ... It's about being able to sell yourself with your voice. We do sessions on appropriate language and how not to speak to people, as well as how to speak to people. It's understanding the impact we have day-to-day through talk and how to speak to people in different situations.'

The perceived need for 'appropriate' language and a 'formal' register as a means to getting on in life relate to the distinction made by Basil Bernstein between 'restricted' and 'elaborated' codes of language. The former refers to non-standard ways of talking understood only by one's immediate social peers, while the latter is a way of communicating beyond this circle and open to universal understanding.[36] While the original view of certain groups in society having access only to a restricted code is no longer helpful, the more general implication for some is that, for all the vibrancy and power of dialects, social mobility may depend on the ability to adopt some form of standardized language. Arguments have been made, for example, for marginalized groups learning how to participate fully in society by learning the 'code of power'.[37]

Nevertheless, there are dangers with this view. Despite its prevalence in current policy in England, standard English is just a small part of a rich and varied daily repertoire of spoken language used even by the most articulate adults. 'Correctness' may become unhelpfully associated, for example, with conventions more suited to *written* language, such as use of full sentences and any stigmatizing of non-standard language also risks undervaluing the potential linguistic assets students bring with them from home. As illustrated in Box 8, perceived issues with home dialects are sometimes more about a mismatch with the somewhat arbitrary conventions of school rather than an inherent deficit.[38]

> **Box 8**
>
> **Research in focus: valuing assets from the home**
>
> In her influential book *Unequal Childhoods*,[39] Annette Lareau painted a vivid picture of the way that language may be experienced differently in the homes of different social groups and of the impact this may have within schools.
>
> Lareau's detailed accounts of a variety of US families shines a light on the way that, in middle-class families, 'concerted cultivation' of their children's development nurtures forms of spoken language likely to be advantageous in a school environment. Parents model rich vocabulary, encouraging and providing opportunities for children to articulate their opinions and to practise verbal skills such as reasoning and negotiating with adults. In homes within lower socioeconomic groups, in contrast, utterances tend to be shorter and more directive, with an assumption that children would not seek to question or negotiate with their elders. In these latter settings, however, Lareau draws attention to the wider assets exhibited by children: non-verbal cues are more important, boundaries and adult authority are respected and, above all, children engage in rich and lively forms of spoken discourse in highly autonomous interactions with their peers. The difference, however, is that the middle-class children's language training in the home is much more aligned to the day-to-day functioning of schools. In school, a broad, specialized vocabulary and the confident public articulation of views are likely to be prized over less formal, but perhaps highly effective, forms of communication.
>
> A question to consider, therefore, is whether, alongside the cultivation of formal modes of talk, in the name of developing cultural capital, there might also be even greater valuing of a more diverse range of spoken language and non-verbal communication, celebrating students' authentic voices.

It has also been argued that any 'policing' of language, often using this metaphor of crime, can be seen as part of a wider agenda of control and standardization rather than as a legitimate goal of learning.[40] The way to reconcile these tensions, therefore, would seem to be an explicit focus on learning to align form with purpose (or register with audience). Returning to the school examples above, we see the teachers attempting to establish this balance. At Rushton, there is a recognition that there are legitimate contexts at school for informal registers that need not be 'corrected', while at Riverside, this is encapsulated in the reference to learning 'how to speak to people in different situations.' It is important, however, that these distinctions do not become too arbitrary and associated merely with different physical settings. Listening to, discussing and valuing a variety of examples of effective talk for different purposes, not just great orators in what can be termed 'final draft', presentational modes,[41] will help students develop proficiency but also judgement in the subtleties of the all-important code-switching needed.

Conversations: listening as well as speaking

Finally, building on the discussion of metacognitive aspects of talk and the awareness of register, this chapter concludes with an often-neglected aspect of this issue: a consideration of audience and interaction. Specifically, this involves learning about conversational turn-taking and the hallmarks of good listening. As the reciprocal counterpart to speaking, it is important to acknowledge that good listening is not a passive experience and that it involves teachable skills meriting a teacher's attention.

Classroom example: Learning to listen

A Year 10 group is in the science lab at Northside beginning a lesson on plant and animal cells. Students sit in pairs, ready to retrieve their prior knowledge, giving the teacher, Rania, a powerful insight into current levels of understanding. In each pair, one student is about to use a diagram as a prompt to tell their partner what they can recall about one of the cell types. Before this sharing begins, however, Rania refers the students to the role of the listener and what might be noticed about the speaker's 'performance': 'Although she [the listener] is listening, she's got to be really focused. Did she [the partner] project? Was she really clear? Did she avoid filler words?'

As the paired talk begins around the room, Rania moves around, eaves-dropping. After a few minutes, the group stops. As well as a summary of the scientific content from a few students who share parts and functions of the different cells, there is simultaneously a focus on the way this content was communicated. Listeners are invited to tell speakers how they did in the task, leading to evaluative comments like 'The information was good, but it could have been a bit slower,' or 'She needed to give eye contact'. Rania asks for a self-assessment of understanding, using coloured pages from a planner and based on this and the talk overheard, moves a few students strategically to work with new partners as the next phase of discussion begins.

Classroom example: ground rules

At Southlea, Year 9 students are about to begin a history lesson. The first part of the lesson will be based largely on dialogue about a contentious issue and students are seated in small groups for this purpose. Before beginning, Isobel is keen to establish some ground rules. 'What is the sort of behaviour we need for debate like this?' she asks. The students make their own suggestions, emphasizing respect for all views. At times, Isobel pushes a little more for a reason, asking why listening is so important, for example. 'So you can think about what someone said and support or refute an argument,' suggests one student.

Having elicited these ideas from past experiences, Isobel reveals a slide on the board with her own simple checklist. As well as the already-discussed points about respect and listening, she draws attention to a third: taking turns. These guidelines are referred to at strategic points in the lesson. Designated talk detectives, building on prompts from an observation proforma, are invited to make connections when evaluating the groups' discussions, while Isobel herself draws attention to the hallmarks of good listening, such as eye contact, just before students present ideas to the class.

In both of these classrooms, the act of listening is given explicit status but the criteria are different, reflecting the purposes of the corresponding talk in each case. In Rania's classroom, the talk centres on a retrieval process. Students need to explain their understanding clearly, not only to consolidate their own memorization, but for the benefit of their partner and also for Rania herself, who has identified a valuable formative assessment opportunity through her eavesdropping. Students' listening and subsequent feedback therefore focuses on both factual content and an audience evaluation of its delivery. Isobel's students, in contrast, are engaged in dialogue around controversial historical issues. Listening has a different function here. It is not about recalling facts but is rather the means to participating meaningfully in the interaction by respecting alternative perspectives and building on previous contributions. This contrast reflects the idea of listening operating at both micro levels (attention to specific points) and macro levels (attention to the bigger picture and subtext).[42] Various strategies can be taught to support this process, corresponding to the planning, monitoring and evaluating aspects of metacognition encountered earlier in the chapter. Students might, for example, decide in advance to focus on specific aspects of what they are hearing, or to make notes as an aid to memory.

A second point that might be taken from these extracts concerns learning about forms of interaction. In the first example, roles are relatively straightforward since one person is designated as an information provider for the other. The history students, however, are engaged in the more complex, fluid task of small-group debate. Note, for example, the explicit reference to ground rules for discussion, including listening and respect for all views. These are agreed in part with the students with discussion around some of the reasons. Mercer refers to such rules as 'common knowledge', which can be invoked by the teacher or the children,'[43] since they become a frame of reference to reiterate at various points. While agreeing ground rules is an important part of creating the conditions for productive talk, it is not unproblematic. Ground rules have been criticized, for example, for having a veneer of negotiation while in reality prescribing middle-class norms as the only acceptable basis for talking[44] and even for undermining the democratic ideals of a dialogic classroom.[45] The assumption of Western conversational conventions, which may require some cultural translation elsewhere in the world has also been noted.[46] While research does establish a correlation between certain talking practices, productive talk and wider attainment,[47] it seems important to try and allow as much authentic negotiation and discussion as possible around ways of talking together. The scaffolds seen in classrooms in this book, such as roles, tokens and stock phrases may be regarded as temporary, therefore, and eventually faded as practices are internalized and more independent interaction takes over.

This chapter has considered some of the ways in which schools lay the foundations for talk-rich classrooms. The chapters to follow will explore the way that these principles are enacted in a variety of learning contexts.

Questions for reflection

- When scaffolding talk, how can you ensure that support is flexible and faded gradually and that responsibility is transferred to the learner?
- When considering the form, content and conduct of spoken language, how do you balance prescription and 'correctness' with the valuing of diversity?
- To what extent should classroom talk strategies be taught discretely versus embedded in the wider curriculum? How would you strike a balance?

Related resources

- The English Speaking Union website offers many resources for formal types of talk such as debates and presentations: https://www.esu.org/resources/
- Voice 21's Listening Ladder is a student-friendly progression of listening skills: https://voice21.org/wp-content/uploads/2020/11/Voice-21-Listening-Ladder.pdf
- Resources for embedding explicit oracy teaching across the curriculum are available at the Tower Hamlets Oracy Hub: https://www.the-partnership.org.uk/school-improvement/oracy-primary

4 Talking with the teacher as a whole class

Chapter preview

Chapter 3 explored some of the strategies used when focusing on learning to talk and listen. This chapter considers how talk can be used productively as a pedagogical tool when working with a whole class. It centres on the teacher's role in orchestrating and creating the conditions for student talk within a class group. Whole-class interaction includes a broad range of teacher talk repertoires, including explanation, modelling and questioning for recall. However, the challenge for teachers is to ensure that this range includes talk that is generative of *thinking*. The chapter covers:

- Insights to frame the practice
- Creating the conditions for productive whole-class talk
- Initiating whole-class talk
- Student participation whole-class talk: an inclusive environment
- Working with student responses: opening up the 'third move'
- Relating spoken to written language

Insights to frame the practice

In more than fifty years of research on spoken language interaction at a class level, the headline findings are clear and remarkably stable over time. Teachers dominate classroom talk and their interaction with students frequently follows a predictable and near-universal pattern. There are good arguments for the teacher's role as an expert being entirely appropriate and often centre-stage in a knowledge-rich curriculum and so it is therefore the *nature and quality* of teacher-student interaction – rather than the ratio – that merits closer inspection.

Throughout a line of studies from the 1960s onwards, teacher talk reigns supreme in classrooms[1] and more recent research suggests that little has changed.[2] There are many possible reasons for this, among them pressures of curriculum coverage and time, worries about loss of control and insecurity about subject knowledge.[3] This state of affairs might raise questions about the ownership of education but the very patterns of teacher-led interaction also have the potential to be cognitively limiting. It ought to be acknowledged that episodes of overtly teacher-led explanation and modelling – heavily reliant on monologic spoken language – are a crucial part of most lessons, but this book's focus is chiefly on talk *involving students*.

It has long been noted that teachers' interactions with their classes around the world and across age groups tend to follow a predictable pattern of initiation–response–feedback (IRF)[4]. The outcome is frequently a rapid, content-based form of questioning and follow-up that guides students in a pre-determined direction, with little time for thought or reasoning, converging on a brief 'correct' answer. Opportunities for students to develop ideas and learn from one another, and for teachers to grasp fully the extent of students' understanding, are therefore missed. While there has been a resurgence of interest in retrieval practice as a means to memorization,[5] questioning in the IRF routine rarely conforms to the systematic approach to participation that this would require. Nevertheless, as Alexander[6] points out in his detailed analysis of talk forms, such 'recitation' has an important place in a teacher's repertoire. The goal, then, may be to add to, rather than supplant, narrow questioning exchanges and many researchers have focused on this very issue.

Considering first of all the questions asked in lessons, extensive research in the US by Martin Nystrand[7] and colleagues points to the power of 'authentic' questions, without a pre-specified answer and therefore allowing for a range of responses. Work by Mercer and others[8] builds on this argument by finding a relationship between academic attainment and what is then *done with* the responses to these more open questions by probing for understanding and encouraging children to articulate their reasoning. This centres on rethinking the third, or feedback, move in the IRF sequence. Mehan and Cazden,[9] for example, suggest that a move 'from recitation to reasoning' is possible by using strategies such as asking for clarification or justification and allowing a number of responses before offering any teacher evaluation. The goal of building chains of more in-depth, articulate reasoned contributions in a cumulative fashion implies a very different – though still active – role for the teacher. Howe's[10] recent work across UK classrooms, for example, shows links between some forms of attainment and particular forms of talk in place of the usual evaluative closing down: firstly, requesting elaboration or clarification and secondly, querying, through expressing challenge, doubt or disagreement. These alternative responses, more generative of powerful student thinking, have been exemplified by Michaels and O'Connor[11] as a set of powerful 'talk moves', such as linking ideas, recapping, noting important points and pressing for reasoning.

Moving into the examples from practice, pay particular attention to:

- how teachers open up questioning
- how teachers allow for meaningful student participation in discussions
- how teachers manage responses, particularly to promote thinking.

Creating the conditions for productive whole-class talk

Before rushing into an exploration of talk in a whole-class context, it is worth reflecting on the distinctive nature of the whole-class forum as a setting for interaction. As noted by a number of commentators, the conventions of classroom talk that we take for granted are actually rather unusual. Tony Edwards,[12] for example, has suggested that student 'competence' in this environment often depends on attributes such as:

- listening to the teacher for long periods
- bidding for the right to speak with just the right amount of enthusiasm
- responding to questions to which the teacher already knows the answer
- having other students' answers accepted as generalized evidence of the class's understanding or misunderstanding
- looking for clues to correct answers in the teacher's cues
- not questioning the lesson content or teacher's expertise
- accepting that one's prior knowledge is unlikely to be taken into account.

While one might take issue with these points individually or collectively as a broad caricature, they are nevertheless likely to be recognizable to some degree as part of the hidden curriculum, as referred to in Chapter 3. Above all, they remind us of some of the routines of interaction – often peculiar to classrooms – into which both students and teachers have been socialized and within, or against which, any new initiatives must work.

Initiating whole-class talk

While teachers' closed questioning for recall has an important place in lessons, not least as a tool for diagnostic assessment at strategic points, research suggests it is unlikely to generate many high-quality or extended student responses.[13] If teachers value student talk in whole-class teaching episodes, the repertoire needs to include, but extend beyond, this sort of 'recitation'. Let's look at two Year 6 classrooms to see this in action.

Classroom example: open questioning for discussion

The answers to the two subtraction calculations on the board at Rushton look initially plausible but contain hidden errors. Amanda's first question to her Year 6 students is a broad one: 'What have you noticed?' She follows up later with 'What is the same and what is different?' At each stage of the ensuing whole-class discussion, open questions are followed by brief paired discussion ('Find some evidence to prove they are wrong. Talk to your partner.') The children have been carefully grouped: the pairs, which will vary from lesson to lesson, are generally mixed attainment but also acknowledge social dynamics, confidence and spoken language skills.

Having collectively identified the errors, the second task focuses on exploring different subtraction methods for problems such as 54,329 subtract 2,481 and 10,632 subtract 997. Again, Amanda's stimulus is open, inviting students to, 'bounce ideas off one another to find an efficient method. At the end, I'm going to get you to explain to us all why it's the most efficient way of doing it.' Armed with mini whiteboards which allow for flexible working and frequent revisions, pairs begin to use exploratory forms of talk ('We could...'; 'What if we...?'; 'Let's try...'), comparing strategies such as counting up, partitioning and subtracting in columns. While the calculation has a single correct answer, Amanda's question about the most efficient method is much more debatable, lending itself to the 'messier' language of hypothesizing, justifying and considering alternatives. Signalling the end of peer discussions, Amanda invites students to convince the class that their method is the most appropriate one. Having just rehearsed this reasoning, there are plenty of volunteers.

The paired and whole-class discussion among these students at the top of the school is the culmination of a longer journey within mathematics lessons. As an early part of Rushton's gradual incorporation of talk across the curriculum, students have become accustomed to starting lessons with 'maths chat', scaffolded at times with sentence stems and talk roles. This has also been a journey for teachers. As the school's oracy lead acknowledges:

'It becomes more about feeding the conversation. It's very easy when you know what you want to share in your head, but just to provide the scaffolding to allow the children to get to that point takes some getting used to. Teachers found that step back difficult at the beginning, letting the children get there themselves, but they are a lot more confident now.'

Classroom example: structure for productive talk

'I'm not going to talk a lot today' says Kate, 'you're going to come up with the ideas, so I don't want to hear too much of my voice.' Year 6 students at Newton have been learning about energy sources. Last week, they made solar ovens from pizza boxes and now Kate wants them to understand the connections between energy and poverty. Today's lesson takes the form of a whole-class discussion of the issues but first there is a reminder of expectations. 'What will we hear today?' she asks. The students suggest that there will be challenging and arguing, as well as agreement. They suggest some useful sentence structures such as, 'I understand what you're saying, but ...'

While the subject matter draws partly on prior learning, Kate wants to ensure that students have something substantive to talk about and has provided various resources to which students can refer. They include graphs of energy use and access to electricity, various statistics relating to the issue and images on the board depicting aspects of poverty. The resources are accompanied by open questions such as, 'What can you say about this graph?' and 'What do you think will happen?'.

Although the focus today is very much on whole-class discussion, Kate breaks down the hour-long lesson into a number of episodes, each prefaced by initial consideration of questions in trios as a way of rehearsing contributions at a class level. Working through these episodes in a structured way, the children progressively discuss issues of energy use, indicators of poverty and then the links between the two. At each stage, the tinkle of wind chime signals that the brief, small-group discussions are giving way to whole-class talk. Although Kate has a clear objective in mind, in terms of establishing the link between energy and poverty, the discussion at each stage is initiated by the students ('Esme's group at the back: you can start us off') and built up cumulatively with openers involving agreeing, disagreeing, adding and building. We will return to Kate's lesson later in this chapter.

Immediately apparent in these two examples are the ways in which both teachers seek to promote thinking through open-ended prompts. At Rushton, Amanda's opener is, 'What have you noticed?' while at Newton, the lesson begins in earnest with, 'What can you say about …?' and 'What do you think will happen?' A sense of curiosity is also promoted, as there is a problem to be solved in both cases: the hidden errors in the maths calculations and the quest for the 'most efficient' method in one lesson and the hidden story about poverty to be found in the data Kate provides in the other.

Questioning is of course a huge topic in its own right and the use of open questioning to provoke and challenge students' thinking is well-established. Taxonomies of question types often associate higher-order thinking with questions requiring responses based on skills like analysis, application and speculation.[14] Speculation, as prompted by 'what if' questions, can involve students asking their own questions too, but it has been noted by David Wood that even open questions from the teacher can inhibit this process by reinforcing the power imbalance in the classroom. He recommends sometimes substituting a personal contribution such as 'I think …' to encourage a more symmetrical dialogue.[15] We can see the beginnings of this speculative mode in Amanda's classroom as the students begin to hypothesize in pairs. Research by Nystrand and others, summarized in Box 9 below, makes a connection between open, 'authentic' questions and attainment. As they emphasize, however, it is ultimately not the form of question itself, or indeed any particular interaction, that is the main issue, but rather the underlying classroom ethos. If such interactions are not to be merely 'pleasant diversions', they suggest, the ultimate test is 'the extent to which instruction requires students to think, not just report someone else's thinking.'[16]

Box 9

Research in focus: 'authentic' questions

Martin Nystrand and colleagues have carried out large-scale analyses of classroom interaction in the US, particularly in English and social studies lessons.[17] They have shown that specific features of interaction are associated with academic gains, most notably:

- authentic questions
- uptake of students' ideas
- opportunities for open discussion.

In many respects, these features correspond to the idea of a dialogic classroom, something we will explore in Chapter 6. Of particular interest here is the concept of an authentic question.

Authentic questions can be contrasted with the much more frequently-encountered recitation questions, which usually test recall of knowledge. Authentic questions are those without a pre-specified answer and which are geared towards promoting thinking, rather than remembering. They do so by deliberately seeking out and exploring differing understandings and views. As well as being generative of open debate, such questions convey a powerful message: this teacher is taking their students seriously and is genuinely interested in their responses.

Although an authentic question is likely to be open and possibly provocative, its authenticity is largely determined not by the wording or structure used, but rather by the teacher's follow-up. The idea of uptake, as another indicator of productive whole-class talk, refers to the way that teachers – or indeed other students – build on initial responses with further questioning, creating a sense of continuity in dialogue. Opening up questioning, then, involves a change in *intent* on the teacher's part and a consideration of what to do with the student response.

Let's take this issue of the wider context around questioning further. The focus so far has been on the teacher's initial prompt, but even the best stimulus can yield either silence or unhelpfully divergent responses. With this in mind, it is possible to discern in these extracts three underlying factors that have helped to create the conditions for productive talk:

1 Despite the apparently open form of interaction, both Amanda and Kate have *clear objectives in mind for the learning* (methods of subtraction and the links between energy and poverty, respectively).

2 The students have sufficient prior knowledge to have *something substantive to* talk *about* (considerable experience of subtraction and prior knowledge about energy, respectively).

3 Before engaging in whole-class discussion, the students are given *opportunities to rehearse their arguments* 'safely' with peers (pairs and small groups, respectively), the dynamics of which will be explored in Chapter 5.

Nystrand and colleagues associate authentic discourse with 'serious instructional goals'[18] and the association of talk-rich pedagogy with curriculum intent is clear in the following account from the head teacher at Underwood.

School example: an ambitious curriculum

'The curriculum was really ambitious and very outward looking, with children having this local to global lens, listening to people speak and having lots of visitors and all these opportunities. But we thought that they knew how to talk, so we were just giving them the opportunities. So it was all there, the curriculum was great: really enabling children to engage with quite complex issues in a meaningful way for them. But, we realized, we stopped and we said, actually do they have the tools to be able to articulate what they're learning effectively, coherently and confidently? No, they don't. So we need the pedagogy, we need to teach them. It was a really great moment when we realized that. It all happened just at the same time so it was perfect.'

The examples so far have touched on some of the ways that students are equipped to respond to teachers' prompts and this is picked up further in the next section.

Student participation in whole-class talk: an inclusive environment

Participation raises questions of inclusive practices for classroom talk. The schools in this book readily provide examples of including all students in talk using a variety of strategies. At small-group level, such strategies might include assigning roles or using tokens as ways of legitimizing participation and preventing others from dominating. At whole-class level, as we have seen already, using very open, accessible questions and fostering a culture of listening are likely to be helpful. As the oracy lead at Woodham puts it:

It comes back to valuing every voice. Every child, whatever they have to contribute, it builds back into the bigger picture of the class discussion and everyone has something to share. So, as a school, we've really welcomed those open questions like, 'What do you notice, what do you see?' It's something that every child can answer at some level.

Nevertheless, there is the danger, as found in the work of Julia Snell and Adam Lefstein,[19] of teachers forming damaging assumptions about 'low ability' learners perceived to be incapable of participating in challenging whole-class talk. At Eastland, the oracy lead counters this view and speaks passionately about adapting practice while maintaining high expectations of all students' participation:

> I'm quite hard line on this. If it was literacy or numeracy, you wouldn't say, if it's hard it's not effective, you'd just think of strategies for those students to access it and you'd scaffold it more. You'd find ways to support them. If you value it, then you teach it and you hold high accountability ... I think there's a bit of a leap there in some teachers' minds to see talk as work to be equal to things like literacy and numeracy and to treat it in the same way. It's an easy one for me: if you value it as work, it's work. We value it and say it's a really key tool to help students progress. They need these skills and therefore let's get them doing it. It's going to be hard and difficult but it's worth it because we see the value in it.

As well as making talk practices themselves inclusive, however, we might also consider how talk is a means to inclusion. With a long-term perspective, this links to the arguments encountered in Chapters 1 and 2 about creating lifelong opportunity. In the shorter term, a focus on spoken language can be seen to provide high-quality *access* to learning for a wider range of students. At Rushton, the reduction of written work in the afternoons has helped some learners in this respect:

> There were children who didn't access learning before because everything was so writing-based but now they know that in the afternoon they have the option to voice record. There's certainly a lot more confidence in our learners with EAL or SEND because they feel they can access it in their own way. That ability to express themselves through speaking has been really powerful.

Meanwhile, at secondary level, 'invisible' students in RE at Riverside have been given a voice:

> It's one of the greatest things we've had for inclusion. We're closing the gaps in RE and I think it's oracy. For example, those 'lost' girls: the ones who sit in the classroom, don't say anything, never cause you any issues, just happily get along. They're the sort of people that you can target now with oracy ... One of the fears with these students has been that I'm going to say it wrong and nobody's going to listen to me. Now these students are being taught how to speak and how to listen.

Some of these inclusive principles can be seen at work in the following classroom examples, which, in different ways, use small-scale talk as a stepping-stone to whole-class sharing.

Classroom example: rehearsing talk in pairs

'Tennis racquets at the ready!' Amy instructs her class at Woodham and pairs of Year 4 students prepare themselves for action. The children are about to engage in virtual serving and volleying of vocabulary ideas to one another as one of a number of interactions with a partner. Words like 'shining', 'twinkling', 'glowing' are knocked rapidly back and forth, with accompanying actions and even grunts, while Amy eavesdrops and scribes some of the emerging ideas on the board at the front of the room.

As a prelude to producing some descriptive writing based on pictures of ancient Egypt, this activity is enabling the class to build up collectively some rich vocabulary and sentence structures on which to draw later. It is primarily a whole-class episode, orchestrated by Amy and including her discussion of individual suggestions and her modelling of writing expanded noun phrases. Nevertheless, a prominent form of interaction is the prefacing of whole-class responses with brief discussion between talk partners. This means that, at each stage in this process of building up verbs and adjectives and refining phrases, every student is an active participant and every student has a receptive audience for their ideas. There is no shortage of volunteers for sharing with the wider class at each point but, as contributions have been rehearsed already (and often overheard through eavesdropping), Amy is equally able to choose students who do not put their hands up, without fear of undue pressure or exposure.

Classroom example: no hands up but a safe space

In Mark's Year 11 PSHE lesson at Eastland, dialogue begins immediately. As students enter, chairs are set out in trios, a seating plan directs them to their group and prompts are ready on the board. The focus of this lesson is making decisions about alcohol and drugs and responding to peer pressure. The provocative talking points include 'Everyone is equal in the eyes of the law' and 'Everyone should try illegal drugs at some point in their life'. A lively exchange of views begins immediately in the small groups.

As the talk gathers pace, Mark circulates and pushes individuals, through his questioning, to clarify or elaborate on their tentative ideas ('So why do you think that is?'). Sometimes he offers a student's views for consideration by a neighbouring group or deliberately over-generalizes to encourage more precise reasoning ('So, you're saying we should definitely all try that?').

As the conversation opens up further to the wider group, it is clear that Mark has high expectations of participation. No hands up are needed, as these students seem accustomed to Mark moving around the room, drawing everyone into the discussion. However, his responses, while challenging, are also non-judgemental and supportive. 'I don't know how to express what I want to say,' claims one student he selects. 'No problem. Can you help her out?' he asks someone else in her group. It is clear that this is a safe space for building and sharing views.

These are contrasting schools and students of very different ages but, in both cases, we can see parallel indicators of a 'safety-net' that allows for high expectations of participation.

1 *Validation*: Talking in pairs or small groups not only allows for the low-stakes rehearsal of ideas noted in the previous section, but also offers students some assurance that their ideas are worthy of attention.
2 *Tuning-in*: Small-scale talk provides an opportunity for the teacher to circulate and eavesdrop on conversations. When students are targeted for an answer, the teacher has the opportunity to choose these contributors in a strategic way, perhaps even referring reassuringly to a good point overheard (this is, of course, rather different from the more systematic calling on students that might be used purely to check understanding).
3 *Peer support*: The whole-class discussions are clearly collective discussions. We see Mark inviting peer support for expressing an idea, while Amy's Year 4 students are able to draw on the rich bank of vocabulary built up by others.

If the goal of teacher–student interaction at whole-class level is primarily to promote recall or gauge understanding, then there are good arguments for a 'no opt-out' culture and the benefits of facilitating responses at these moments by extending 'wait time' after asking a question are well documented.[20] However, we should consider a little more deeply our assumptions about participation where *thinking* is the prime goal. Lefstein and Snell have shown, through close analysis of classroom episodes, the subtleties of drawing students into more dialogic interactions.[21] As well as responding to raised hands, teachers such as Amy and Mark use their knowledge of individuals to notice a multitude of cues – sometimes non-verbal – signalling students' potential for making a contribution, even when this has not been overtly offered.

As noted in Chapter 1, with its mention of 'exuberant voiceless participation',[22] contributions can vary in quality. While the collective academic and social benefits of talk-rich classrooms are well-established,[23] the evidence around individual participation is more inconclusive: some research has established a link between individual contributions and attainment,[24] but there is often a more ambiguous picture. Some studies, for example, suggest that silent students may learn just as much as their more vocal peers – though this depends on a culture of active, engaged listening, which needs to be cultivated.[25] They also remind us that students' silence may have many reasons, sometimes linked to attainment levels, which require very different teacher responses to evaluate their signals and facilitate their involvement.[26] The following brief example from Northside offers an interesting perspective on participation.

This glimpse of a maths lesson calls into question what counts as whole-class participation. At first glance, this is a teacher working extensively with just one student at the expense of spreading the interaction more widely. Viewed another way, however, we can see the selected student reasoning on behalf of the group. His moment in the spotlight is carefully supported by Mo and his peers are called upon to verify or offer alternatives as appropriate. Meanwhile, teacher and student model working through a problem through their thinking aloud.

Chapter 2 referred to Alexander's 'five cultures' research.[27] The classroom episode from Northside is reminiscent in some ways of what was found in Russian classrooms. In contrast to a preoccupation with distributing questions and interacting briefly with as many students as possible, Alexander noted that Russian teachers often worked intently with a single student as a representative of the others. Participation for the others meant watching and listening: 'For the moment, that child is the class and all are participating.'[28] As in this example of Mo's lesson, Alexander noted that lower-attaining students were just as likely to be selected, not with any form of public test in mind but to emphasize that we learn from and build on our own mistakes as an essential part of learning.

From these contrasting examples and the ensuing discussion, perhaps there is a particular understanding of participation and inclusion to take forward. Participation for the purpose of *thinking* (as opposed to formative assessment) is not gauged by the number of students responding. It is better understood as a collective endeavour that depends as much on a culture of active listening as on vocal contribution.

Working with student responses: opening up the 'third move'

In the typical back-and-forth of whole-class interaction, there is much to gain by focusing on what could be called the 'third move', or the teacher's response to a student's contribution. As previously noted, this part of an initiation–response–feedback (or evaluation) sequence is often where the dialogue is closed down, as the teacher offers a brief evaluative comment before moving on. This moment, however, is a powerful one if utilized effectively and the frequent use of 'feedback', rather than 'evaluation', as a term for this third move hints at broader possibilities.[29] The following examples, spanning different age groups and schools, illustrate some of the potential follow-ups.

Classroom example: a teacher's follow-up questions

At Brookfield, James's Year 7 mathematics students are going over some questions related to calculating the perimeter of shapes. They have already attempted the questions independently but, rather than a simple confirmation of correct answers, this is an opportunity for discussion. James selects two questions for particular focus.

The first is a relatively simple calculation, but likely to lead to careless errors. Rather than leading with a straightforward question, James leads, more provocatively, with a question based on an error. 'Some people have said the perimeter is 16 cm,' James says. 'What are they missing?' After some brief paired discussion, students offer explanations. Although most are correct, James probes further by offering plausible but incorrect alternatives such as, 'Hmm, why not 32?'.

The second perimeter question features a rectilinear shape with some missing measurements. Again, a problem is posed. 'It seems like there's not enough information,' ponders James aloud. As students begin to suggest strategies, there are follow-up questions. Some are directed to the student answering, either to elicit clarification through elaboration ('And how did that idea help you to work it out?') or to push for greater precision through deliberate misinterpretation: 'Oh, so you mean I could do this?' he says, sketching the shape with the wrong measurements.

At other times, James follows up by offering a student's idea back to the rest of the class for consideration. 'What's another way of explaining that to somebody?' he asks at one point. In response to another student's suggested strategy, he feigns confusion, asking 'What does she mean and how does that help?'. This leads to a flurry of work on mini whiteboards as students sketch the shape in question as a tool for articulating their reasoning to a neighbour and ultimately to the wider group.

Classroom example: challenging students' answers

We are back in Kate's Year 6 classroom at Newton Primary, as the students' consideration of energy and poverty moves forwards. Superficially, this is a student-led discussion and part of the school's quest to empower the children to equip themselves with knowledge as well as relying on the teacher. However, Kate is far from being a passive bystander in the process. Firstly, she frequently pushes for further detail: 'Is there some evidence to back up your argument?'; 'Explain more about that'; 'What defines a poor country, then?'. She is also alert to the need to challenge assumptions and stereotypes: 'So you're saying homelessness leads to criminality. All the time?'; 'When you just referred to Africa, did you mean all of Africa?'. As part of this role as challenger, Kate feeds provocative points into the discussion at appropriate moments. As well as her own statements, Kate's eavesdropping and participation during the small-group talk has tuned her in to some useful starting points ('Hot countries don't need much electricity. That's Hamza's conjecture. What do the rest of you think?'). Provocations also occur in the form of children's questions to the wider class. 'Why can't someone in poverty just get a job?' asks Corey, leading instantly to a host of responses from his classmates.

Through this process, with its rigorous appeal to reasoning and evidence, initial ideas are valued but also probed, challenged and often refined. The class conception of poverty, for example, evolves from centring mainly on people in 'poor countries', or the local homeless, to a broader understanding of relative poverty and lack of opportunity. Energy, similarly, becomes understood as a gateway not only to heat and light but also to clean water and education. As the class's thinking develops collectively, Kate summarizes: 'So I think we've agreed that poverty can be anywhere and is about access to something?' She reinforces this developing understanding by returning to a student and asking whether their earlier views have stayed the same or changed, asking: 'So, Ella, what do you think now?'

Towards the end, one student sums up her thinking in a personal manifesto. 'I feel like there should be solar panels for all new houses if we are going to stop world pollution,' she states passionately. There is a vote of confidence from a classmate: 'Wow, that's great. You should be on the news!'

As shown in Box 10 and corroborated in other studies,[30] research suggests that participation involving elaboration and querying is especially associated with attainment gains.

Box 10

Research in focus: dialogue and attainment

In an example of a large-scale correlational study, exploring the relationship between attainment and features of talk between teachers and students, Christine Howe and colleagues examined naturally-occurring classroom interaction from 72 classrooms in 48 UK primary schools.[31] They found three features of dialogue to be positively associated with high attainment in mathematics and English tests (though not with science and reasoning):

- Participation
- Elaboration
- Querying.

In essence, *High student participation* in dialogue involving *elaboration* and *querying* was found to be a potent combination.

High participation involved multiple students expressing ideas publicly and at length, while also engaging with the ideas of others. Elaboration and querying, usually instigated by the teacher, were exemplified by prompts such as, 'Who would like to build on ...?' and 'Do you really think that ...?'. The presence of *these three features together* seemed to create an environment in which individuals' ideas were interconnected, made explicit and considered alongside alternatives. The researchers speculated that the impact on attainment was due, therefore, to the creation of metacognitive conditions in which students could 'watch themselves think'.

A follow-up study involving analysis of the same data zoomed in on the hallmarks of classrooms with the highest quality dialogue and the highest attainment in an effort to explore further the preconditions for success.[32] Common features included: planned-for talk-intensive tasks; the use of shared objects, or resources, as a focus for talk and the teachers' creation of a culture of openness, withholding their own judgement and encouraging alternative student views (sometimes rehearsed with peers before sharing).

Elaboration and querying can simply involve appropriate follow-up questions, such as asking for clarification and justification. One striking feature of these two examples, however, is the way that the teachers achieve this by adopting a gently sceptical or provocative role. In the mathematics classroom, we see James not only starting with a focus on an error but at times feigning confusion or deliberately misinterpreting an answer. In doing so, he pushes for precision and clarity. If James's tone is puzzled, then Kate's is often challenging as she probes for evidence and seizes on generalizations, sometimes turning questions back on the class. In both cases, the message is clear: vague, unsubstantiated responses will not do in these classrooms. The stance of these two teachers has much in common with a Socratic style of dialogue in which, through a process of guided inquiry, ideas are subjected to critical scrutiny. It has been noted, however, that this process of challenge and disagreement involves a degree of interpersonal and emotional challenge within the classroom,[33] further underlining the importance of creating a culture of openness referred to in Box 10. At Newton, for example, Kate is a highly experienced teacher and lessons such as this one have been filmed so that other colleagues can reflect on the subtleties of this style of interaction.

Also notable in the extracts is the role played by the teachers as orchestrators of the discussion. Mercer has identified 'cohesive devices' such as recaps, repetitions and reformulations of students' views.[34] Essentially, this is about keeping the class on the same page. We see this in action above, for example, in the way that James draws attention to strategies that have helped with the shape calculations ('And how does that help?') and the way that Kate summarizes the emerging and evolving views on poverty ('So I think we've agreed that …'). Such interventions in an evolving discussion align with the 'teacher moves' referred to by Sarah Michaels and colleagues.[35] They include: marking important points; challenging students by redirecting questions or offering counter-examples; modelling strategies by making thinking public and recapping where the discussion has got to. In these ways, James and Kate can be seen to be regulating the thought process on behalf of the class as a form of collective metacognition. A collective approach to meaning-making can also be seen with these younger learners at Downland.

Classroom example: thinking collectively.

In the purpose-built science laboratory, Nathan's Year 3 children are learning about light. Although the lesson includes Nathan's demonstration of phenomena such as opaque objects blocking light to create shadow, it is clear from the 'Orac-sci' posters on the wall that this is a learning environment in which student talk is valued too.

The lesson centres on a picture book, *Fox in The Night*, which lends itself to exploring scientific issues. Children are asked to consider questions such as whether it is ever completely dark at night in the city or what sources of light can be seen in each picture. At these moments, rather than questions put to individuals, small groups seated around their science benches are first asked to have brief discussions. When answers are shared, they are built up collectively. Responding students do not find their answers immediately evaluated and closed off but are asked to nominate a peer to add to what has gone before ('Choose who you would like to carry on our conversation'). If a student is reticent about selecting someone, Nathan supports them by modelling the question for the child to repeat: 'Abdur, is there anything you would like to add to our discussion? That would be a nice way to bring someone in.'

As the school's oracy lead notes, changing to more open forms of whole-class discussion represents a transition for some practitioners but:

'The results are so lovely and, in some respects, it makes a teacher's job easier if you can have conversations where all children are contributing. It's easier to teach a more engaged class than trying to get blood out of a stone.'

This collective dimension to these whole-class discussions is also worthy of consideration. The importance of participation and active involvement in engaging with ideas raised has been established above[36] and is clear in all three examples. James prompts his students to explain their thinking to one another, as they build a shared understanding, while questions and ideas raised by individuals in Kate's class are offered to the wider group for consideration. With the younger children in Nathan's science lesson, we see a more structured form of collective thinking as students are explicitly taught to invite their peers to build on previous contributions. Greeno has shown how moving beyond a closed third move can position the student differently in relation to the class and the teacher.[37] For example, rather than initiation–response–feedback (IRF), consider the following.

- *IRQA*: The teacher asks a further question about the first response and students become attuned to an initial response being not a definitive statement, but an idea that will be expanded upon. In the first example, we see James responding to a correct answer not with an affirmation but the question, 'Why not …?'
- *IRRF*: The teacher re-voices a response and the fourth move is then taken by a student. In the second example, Kate re-voices Hamza's view on hot countries and electricity, offering it back to the class for evaluation with, 'What do the rest of you think?'

So far, this chapter has focused on whole-class talk as a learning episode in its own right, but some of the extracts also relate to written work. The final section considers the relationship between talking in the whole-class forum and written forms of language.

Relating spoken to written language

The relationship between spoken and written language is not necessarily straightforward. Ronald Carter's work, for example, reinforces the points made in Chapter 3 about differing criteria for quality by emphasizing that spoken – and particularly conversational – language has a grammar of its own, one that is potentially much richer than its written counterpart.[38] While it will be clear by now that this book treats classroom talk as much more than a stepping-stone towards a written 'main event', the case for spoken language proficiency informing writing has been made frequently.[39] Two brief examples from Queensway show us this in action.

Classroom example: oral rehearsal

Cathy prepares her class: 'OK everybody, from the top, really clearly. Use your actions to help you remember.' Year 2 students are building up to writing instructions about how to feed a dragon. Based on previously drawn sketches of this feeding process, children work through the steps as instructions, using agreed actions. The instructions have been chunked in small sections and at each stage these are performed to a partner as a rehearsal ('I want one person to speak and the other just to listen') before returning to the whole-class choral rendition. All the children join in with loud, confident voices and obvious enjoyment. Their spoken lines begin with imperative – or 'bossy' – verbs, emphasized by exaggeration in their intonation: 'Did you hear the way she said it?' notes Cathy, 'That was the important bit.'

Classroom example: evaluating writing

Meanwhile, along the corridor, Year 5 and 6 classes are working on relative clauses. As they read chorally, intonation, as in Year 2, is varied for effect to highlight these clauses. Whole-class consideration of ideas is interspersed frequently with paired talk: partners discuss sentences based on the text of *A Christmas Carol*, identifying the clauses together and then suggesting their own constructions that might be added to enhance, or 'upgrade', more basic sentences. Supported by previously created character adjectives sheets, ideas are tried out on mini whiteboards, allowing for a provisional form of thinking and revision. Questioning from one of the teachers, Kelly, guides the interaction, which at different times might focus on content or form: 'Read the sentences to your partner. Are they about the same thing?' 'Who has an example with a really good word choice?'

Unlike the emphasis in previous sections on stimulating new ideas and understanding, here we see talk serving a different purpose. It appears to be supporting writing in three powerful ways that may be generalizable to other contexts:

1 *Allowing a focus purely on content.* In these examples, this concerns the conventions for using instructions or relative clauses, both in terms of form (such as imperative verbs and relative pronouns) and substantive content. Being initially unencumbered by aspects of written work such as correct spelling potentially reduces the demands on working memory and allows for the inclusion of students for whom writing presents particular challenges.

2 *Internalizing linguistic structures.* The choral rehearsal of what will later become written language also allows for unfamiliar linguistic structures to be internalized through hearing and speaking these constructions. In this respect, the Year 2 lesson in particular has the hallmarks of the Talk for Writing approach popularized by Pie Corbett, in which students experience an 'imitation' stage drawing on text maps, drama and oral rehearsal.[40]

3 *Promoting dialogue about writing.* In the Year 5 and 6 classroom, we see an additional post-drafting process at work. Kelly is using the whole-class forum, interspersed with paired work, to engage students in what has been called 'metatalk'.[41] This involves making visible some of a writer's decisions, such as vocabulary choice in this case, and sometimes going beyond prescription to evaluate possibilities in a dialogic way.

It is important to note at this point the *reciprocity* between these forms of language and the fact that the written may precede the spoken. Examples involving Year 6 and Year 8 students' analysis of texts have been encountered already (Chapter 1 and 3, respectively) but let's take a closer look at this with younger students at Fairway.

Classroom example: responding to a story

Sandy's Year 2 class is enjoying the picture book *Izzy Gizmo* by Pip Jones and Sara Ogilvie. Sandy reads the book to the class, bringing the story to life with exuberant voice and gesture. For all her engaging storytelling, however, Sandy's is not the only voice in this lesson. At one point, she is keen to help the children make sense of an incident involving shredded wallpaper and the mention of 'confetti' as a potentially unfamiliar word. 'What happened to the wallpaper?' she asks, 'Turn, talk and tell!' Animated paired discussion breaks out and students then offer their interpretations to the rest of the class. As the class comes to a shared understanding, there are gasps as the scene is brought to life with confetti 'magically' tumbling from the pages of Sandy's book. The story progresses and paired talk is used once again to consider how a particular character might be feeling. With a reminder to face whoever is speaking, Sandy brings the class back together and this time asks for sharing in the form of a single adjective each ('No repeating!). With pace and energy, ideas are fired from around the room, including 'despondent' and 'flabbergasted'. 'Have any of you ever felt like that when something didn't work?' asks Sandy.

Talk in this case is being used for comprehension purposes, but this also involves elaboration on what is in the text, as additional details and emotions are inferred and new vocabulary suggested. The collective response therefore positions students as both current readers and future writers. As the next chapter moves towards peer dialogue specifically, this example serves as a reminder more generally that learning to talk, even in the most formal sense, necessarily involves an audience; that audience, whether teacher or peers, creates a moment of potential dialogue and interaction.

Questions for reflection

- What proportion of questioning in your classroom consists of 'authentic', as opposed to 'test', questions? Is that proportion appropriate?
- How do you go about encouraging participation in whole-class discussions, balancing a supportive culture with high expectations of participation?
- What could you do to create a culture of active listening and participation that need not always involve speaking?

Related resources

- This Oracy Cambridge blog by Wendy Lee considers students with SLCN and the benefits of oracy for inclusion: https://oracycambridge.org/how-inclusive-is-oracy/
- Cult of Pedagogy offers some formats and practical strategies for whole-class discussion: https://www.cultofpedagogy.com/speaking-listening-techniques/
- Edutopia's video shows talk moves in action: https://www.edutopia.org/video/encouraging-academic-conversations-talk-moves

5 Talking with peers

Chapter preview

While the previous chapter focused primarily on whole-class interaction, another familiar context for classroom talk is small-group peer discussion, as students work more independently. This can be as simple as a brief exchange in a pair or may involve more sustained group work. The common thread in every case, however, is the need to create the conditions for purposeful talk. This chapter covers:

- Insights to frame the practice
- Understanding the potential benefits of learning through peer talk
- Creating the conditions for productive peer talk
- Facilitating peer talk: the teacher as an active participant
- Drawing the elements together: a teacher's account

Insights to frame the practice

Talk among students is a thorny issue. For some, it is associated with concerns about off-task behaviour, exemplified by accounts of a government minister's fears of 'idle chatter' in the classroom.[1] For others, championing direct instruction as a preferred means for the transmission and retention of knowledge, there may be connotations with unproductive group work.[2] What seems clear is that students talking together does not automatically lead to productive learning. Certain conditions need to be in place. It is important, therefore, to examine both the potential benefits of peer-to-peer talk but also the strategies essential for its success.

There is an extensive body of research into various models of peer-to-peer talk which attests to its potential for transferable gains for reasoning, but also for attainment in various curriculum areas. This evidence comes from programmes such as Thinking Together,[3] Collaborative Reasoning[4] and Reciprocal Teaching.[5] What all these approaches share is a high level of structure that promotes particular forms of spoken language. Building on the work of Douglas Barnes,[6] Neil Mercer and colleagues have written and researched at length on 'exploratory talk' as an especially productive form of collaborative language. This is characterized by dialogue in which participants 'engage critically but constructively with each other's ideas', such that 'knowledge is made publicly accountable, and reasoning is visible in the talk.'[7] Through appropriation of strategies or knowledge, co-construction of new ideas and transformation of one's own thinking at a metacognitive level, peers talking in this way can 'interthink' and perform a scaffolding function for one another.[8]

Although the quality of thinking, rather than an efficient group work output, is often the main goal, attaining this high level of collaborative talk nevertheless relies upon careful preparation. A great deal of this is down to the explicit teaching of the requisite skills, both in terms of 'ground rules' for collaboration and specific language structures that facilitate dialogue.[9] Additionally, the nature of the task is all-important: fruitful tasks for talk must have a degree of openness and challenge but also be set up to require diverse, contrasting perspectives from a small group of participants.[10] While the emphasis is on peer-to-peer talk, the teacher's role is significant. As well as the preparatory groundwork, interventions to model and prompt appropriate verbal interaction can be powerful.[11] A final consideration is the careful use and timing of peer dialogue as part of a wider learning experience. The importance of group members having a degree of expertise in the subject matter – in other words, bringing with them some prior knowledge – is likely to be a prerequisite for deeper thought and effective collaboration.[12]

Issues for attention in the examples that follow might centre around:

- the particular features of children's language that seem most productive
- the teacher's preparatory work in teaching students how to talk together and ensuring prior knowledge of the subject matter
- the kinds of tasks that facilitate productive peer talk
- the teacher's active role during peer discussion tasks.

Understanding the potential benefits of learning through peer talk

Before considering how to create the conditions for productive peer talk, it is important to make a case for why this is worthwhile in the first place. After all, isn't asking students to learn from and with one another a recipe for distraction, off-task behaviour and the perpetuation of misconceptions? Certainly, there are many episodes within learning which need to be teacher-led, as new ideas are explained and modelled. However, when sequenced and set up appropriately, peer talk has the potential to add distinctive value. In terms of individual benefits, some of this relates to ideas, derived from the work of Lev Vygotsky,[13] of a student as 'more knowledgeable other' helping a peer to go a little further than they might independently. This process, related to the scaffolding discussion in Chapter 3, is one of the points alluded to by these students from Woodham.

Listening to learners: learning from and with others

Year 4 students, reflecting on working with their peers are able to identify various benefits. They explain, for example, that talking with a partner or small group is useful because, 'If you can't understand something, the person next to you can tell you.' Similarly, it can serve to initiate thinking as, 'talk can help give other people ideas if they don't know how to start.' Peer talk is also a safe space to rehearse ideas for later public sharing as, 'If you're stuck it gives you time to think about what to say,' and provides as ready audience for each person because, 'If you can share your ideas with a talk partner, you don't feel left out because sometimes people don't let you speak.' Finally, this sort of interaction can help the smooth running of the classroom as, 'the teacher can't solve everyone's problems so your partner can help instead.'

What can also be taken from these views, however, is a hint of another of Vygotsky's insights, seen in the references to sharing ideas and having 'time to think of what to say'. This is the idea that language fulfils not only an external, communicative function but is also a way of organizing and internalizing one's thoughts. While this theory suggests important cognitive, affective and organizational outcomes, it also implies a hierarchical relationship between either students of differing expertise levels or between the teacher as problem-solver and a student as a rather passive participant. While these asymmetrical relationships are a feature of classrooms, peer talk also has the potential for a more symmetrical co-construction of understanding. Partly, this is based on a culture of mutual respect in the face of disagreement, as seen in comments from Year 7, 8 and 9 students at Fairway.

Listening to learners: 'friendly arguments'

'[Group discussion] helps us a lot because we get to hear our peers' opinions and we get to learn more and it gets into an argument, but a friendly argument.'

'In a friendly argument, if a person disagrees with what you just said, you can nod and say, "Oh yeah, I understand" and you make the other person feel you didn't take it the wrong way and it then helps other people to disagree.'

'In these friendly arguments, we don't think anyone's wrong to say anything. They can support their idea. If someone's disagreeing with them, they can defend the argument and support the idea and why they were saying it. Then someone can agree with it or challenge it. When challenging it, they might say, "Well you said this, but what about that?" It helps us to arrange what we say.'

Fairway's 'friendly arguments' depend on an openness to alternative perspectives. Mercer uses the concept of an 'intermental development zone' (IDZ) to describe a dynamic space for thinking together. It involves an active role for students as they work with others in a shared communicative mode[14] and links to the related and powerful idea of 'interthinking' or thinking collectively through the use of language.[15] The following extract shows some of this collective thought at work.

Classroom examples: exploring mathematics

Students in Year 9 mathematics at Brookfield sit facing one another around a table in mixed-attainment groups. Each student has a mini whiteboard to help them explain their thinking to others and Adam, the teacher, emphasizes the importance of articulating reasoning rather than recording final answers. One group begins to consider this afternoon's first question, which asks how many significant figures a particular number might have been rounded to.

Ben: There's a range it could be.

Liam: Well, if it's three, it could be from 1000 ... so the highest would be [writes on board].

Jan: What I'm looking at now is this [indicates on board].

Liam: I know when you round to a significant figure you normally don't use zero.

Ben: So, let's say it was four significant figures, it would be this [writes on board]. So, Amy, do you agree? If it was four significant figures, it would be this? [draws for Amy].

Amy: Yes, OK.

Liam: So, basically, it could be three or four then?

Ben: Well, I'd say four [writes on board].

Liam: Let's see what you've got there. So, the smallest it can be is this and the biggest is this [showing board].

Jan: Amy, what's the highest possible that would round to that number? Remember, if it ends in 4 it rounds down, 5 rounds up.

Amy: Mmm. Not sure.

Liam: [shows Amy his board] So, basically, these are the significant figures underlined. So, do you see how that makes sense?

The use of mini whiteboards as a tool for discussion is a consistent feature of work in Adam's classroom. As he explains:

'Collectively working on whiteboards, rubbing things out, removes all fear of failure from the question because it can just be erased from all record ... In a lot of subjects, you have this planning phase, like in English you quite often for essays spend half an hour planning something and then pull all your ideas together and then write it out. In maths, it's almost like you're meant to somehow see the four steps down the line. And a lot of kids just can't process that ... So for me, it represents that planning phase where they can work collectively and put their heads together, have all this messy thinking working out.'

Elsewhere in the room, a little further into the same lesson, a pair of students has moved on working on laptops to apply these rounding principles to calculating error intervals.

Rav: It's not a multiple of 50.

Jamie: Look, if this is 201, then it would go up, wouldn't it?

Rav: But look at this. It says greater than.

Jamie: Well, what do you think it would be?

Rav: It would be bigger.

Jamie: Doesn't have to be bigger [draws on board]. Look at this line. It's to the nearest ten. So, we put 400 in the middle and go up ten and down ten, right?

Rav: OK, so let's check that. I'm not sure. Let's see if we can get this [types answer into computer].

In these extracts, we glimpse ideas emerging as an outcome of students' dialogue. There is a sense that the small-group interactions may have generated some understanding beyond that held by each individual beforehand. In the first extract, for example, there are speculative contributions from Ben which help to open up the question in terms of possibilities, helpful summing up of key understanding from Liam and attempts to share current thoughts with Amy towards the end. While there is little challenge or dispute here, the second brief extract sees Rav and Jamie questioning one another's assumptions about the problem. Through a lively but constructive dialogue, they clarify, check and refine their strategies.

This constructive, generative and respectful form of dialogue has some hallmarks of what has been called 'exploratory talk'. Exploratory talk has been characterized and distinguished from others in terms of its audience and its mode of interaction. Originally, Douglas Barnes distinguished exploratory speech from what he termed 'final draft' speech.[16] Whereas final draft speech is aimed at an external audience and is therefore likely to be planned and somewhat polished, exploratory talk is a working tool, spontaneous and purely for the group's internal consumption. As a result, Barnes explains exploratory talk as follows: 'Talk here is a means for controlling thinking … I call this groping towards a meaning exploratory talk. It is usually marked by frequent hesitations, rephrasings, false starts and changes of direction.'[17]

In this messy form of talk, contributions are tentative and hypothetical. Another important definition of exploratory talk is associated with Mercer and colleagues who contrast it with disputational and cumulative talk.[18] Disputational talk is marked by disagreement and competition, while cumulative talk sees an uncritical acceptance of others' ideas. Both are likely to be educationally unproductive compared with exploratory talk, in which there are reasoned arguments, consideration of different points of view, constructive engagement with peers and often an informed consensus as an outcome.

It will probably be no surprise that exploratory talk, perhaps through 'friendly arguments', is relatively rare in most classrooms and can be difficult to nurture. The next section will consider how the optimal conditions can be created, but why is it specifically this form of peer talk that is most prized? Apart from the arguments for student voice and participation touched on in Chapter 1, evidence from many research studies associates exploratory talk with gains in not only reasoning but also attainment in external tests.[19] This impact was explained in Box 2 from Chapter 1 as the result of three processes[20] and we can now see them at work in the extracts from Adam's class:

1 *Appropriation*: Learners share useful information and strategies in their discussions. Ben, Jan and Liam explain their thinking to Amy to ensure a shared understanding within the group.
2 *Co-construction*: Students build on their peers' thoughts so that the group becomes more than the sum of its parts. Rav and Jamie question one another's assumptions and their disagreement leads them to realize that they need to check their answer.
3 *Transformation*: The group's reasoning process can become internalized at an individual level, strengthening a student's subsequent independent thinking. In both extracts, students introduce useful strategies including hypothesizing ('Let's say it was ...') and using drawings to visualize a problem ('Look at this line ...'). These tools for thinking are then potentially part of every student's repertoire for future problem-solving.

Through the lens of cognitive science and ideas of cognitive load, there is also a suggestion that a well-designed small-group experience can create a form of collective working memory, giving a group more capacity than a collection of individuals.[21] The recaps for Amy in the first extract serve, for example, as markers for everyone of where the thinking has got to. While we can therefore identify some features of productive talk in Adam's lesson, this has not occurred by chance, arising instead from an interplay of factors relating to shared expectations, the type of task and Adam's own role in the process. Let's now look more closely at these conditions.

Creating the conditions for productive peer talk

Asking people of any age to talk and think together can easily be unproductive and it is not difficult to see why some teachers may seek the relative security of teacher-led instruction. The contention here, however, is that an alternative to simply rejecting this approach is to understand *how*, and *when*, to use peer talk. Much of its success depends on the task itself: more specifically the way it is structured for students and where it falls in a sequence of learning. In the large-scale analyses of Nystrand and Gamoran,[22] for example, working in small groups was actually often associated with *lower* achievement. This outcome was largely related to inappropriate task choice, however. Effective peer collaboration, they suggest, depends on tasks that are somewhat open-ended, that offer a degree of autonomy and that require a sharing of perspectives and the co-construction of understanding.

Chapter 4 illustrated instances of talk in pairs interspersed with whole-class interaction. The following two examples, one from a primary and one from a secondary classroom, illustrate the more complex scenario of small-group talk, contrasting a partly teacher-led task with a more independent one.

Classroom example: providing structure and purpose for group talk: primary

At Newton, guided reading in Year 6 is based on a book that each child reads independently in preparation for the session. This pre-session work promotes reading at home and allows for a discussion of longer extracts. It also means that guided reading time can be wholly devoted to informed dialogue arising from this week's assigned chapter. Currently, students are reading Onjali Rauf's *The Boy at the Back of the Class*, its tale of refugees resonating with the experiences of some of the readers in this school. As their classmates read independently, six students settle around a table for half an hour's high-quality discussion with their teacher, Maria.

First of all, Maria reminds the students briefly of the conventions for talking in this group: they are to indicate with their thumbs when they have a contribution and should avoid talking over one another. Although turn-taking is important, debate and challenge are expected here. 'I really like it when you challenge each other and disagree', says Maria, 'but we have ways of doing this politely.' To support the process, she passes round sheets with helpful sentence stems for challenging, agreeing, encouraging, instigating and summarizing and gives a few moments for them to be read and understood.

With that, the discussion begins and Maria provokes a first exchange of views by asking about the impact of the narrator remaining anonymous. Very quickly, thumbs go up and ideas are shared between students. Calling on any quieter students, she invites elaboration throughout using open-ended prompts such as, 'So you think ...?' and 'Why is that ...?' As the children build on each other's ideas with openers like, 'While I understand Abdul's point, I think ...', Maria introduces new specialist vocabulary to assist in their evaluation of character roles, explaining and modelling the use of words like protagonist, antagonist, dynamic and static.

In due course, the group turns to a second form of interaction as Maria highlights a dilemma faced by the characters and uses this as the stimulus for a SWOT (strengths, weaknesses, opportunities and threats) analysis. The scenario under discussion involves a visit to the queen, with reference to the changing of the guard at the palace. Recognizing that changing the guard is likely to be outside the lived experiences of the children and a form of unfamiliar cultural 'literacy', Maria shows a brief film clip to illustrate this tradition. Armed with this knowledge, the six students break into two smaller groups of three to consider the issue. They use a SWOT sheet to make rough notes ready to share but Maria emphasizes, 'Don't worry too much about the writing. We just need to talk right now.'

After a few minutes, the six reconvene and, with just minimal prompting, they share some thoughts and underlying reasoning about the characters' choices. As Maria explains later, having the confidence to build on others' views and share their thinking is part of this school's wider vision for developing cultural capital and breaking the 'glass ceiling' of opportunity for their students.

Classroom example: providing structure and purpose for group talk: secondary

Year 9 students at Southlea enter Isobel's history classroom to find an unfamiliar seating plan. Most students have been allocated places in groups of four, while others are individually placed on the fringes of these groups. The reason for this soon becomes apparent, as Isobel explains that this will be a 'fishbowl' debate: each table will consider interpretations of Germany's defeat in World War Two, while an onlooker, as a talk detective, notes discussion features.

Isobel is one of three staff members at Southlea working as a pioneer on classroom talk and providing a support for her colleagues. Students in this class are used to talking, not least because this unit of study, like all others, has at least one oral assessment point. To support the interaction, each table has a sheet offering possible talk roles or tactics – such as probing, challenging and summarizing – along with related sentence starters. With the mode of engagement clarified, and reminders about respectful discussion issued, the other precursor to the debate is to ensure that contributions will be well-informed. Students are provided with a number of written sources pertaining to the topic and given ten minutes to read them and highlight potentially useful information, ensuring, as Isobel puts it, that, 'you'll have all the evidence at your fingertips when you start talking'. The talk detectives, meanwhile, are briefed to note on structured record sheets not only good arguments made, but also examples of interaction and participation.

Having decided on a student to act as the instigator, groups begin their dialogues. The students are left to talk largely independently but there is a tight time limit for this initial episode of talk. Different ideas are offered and relevant evidence from the readings on issues such as supply chains and strategic decisions are cited. After five minutes or so, before attention begins to wane, Isobel stops the conversations. There is time for a quick reflection on the content and conduct of the debate so far and a reminder that talk detectives need to prepare to feed back.

After this brief interlude, a new, more provocative statement is fed in as a talking point, taking the dialogue to a new level: 'If Hitler had been assassinated in 1940, Germany would have won the war.' There is an immediate buzz of interest as animated conversations resume. This time, Isobel lets the discussion run for just over ten minutes before interjecting with another plenary phase. 'What was successful about what you heard? Who had a really good discussion and why?' she asks the talk detectives. Referring to the discussion guidelines from the start of the lesson and the prompts on their sheets, the detectives cite specific features they have observed. Group members also feed back on their ideas but, here too, Isobel is interested in the form of the interaction as well as its content: 'What consensus did you reach? Is consensus important in a discussion?'

In these classrooms, despite contrasts in school context, education phase, year group and subject, we can nevertheless see several aspects of commonality. Beginning with the underlying substance of the discussions, it is important to recognize that talk needs to be purposeful or, put more starkly, students need something to talk *about*. The kind of exploratory talk aspired to in the previous section often involves a degree of critical thinking and Daniel Willingham[23] has argued for the importance of domain knowledge as a prerequisite for this. This in turn raises the question of peer talk's place in a sequence of learning. While talk between students can be highly beneficial at the start of a topic as a way of eliciting prior knowledge, for engaging interest or for opening up lines of enquiry, the talk in these extracts has a different purpose. In both cases, these lessons involve informed debate requiring some underlying substance. As a result, the examples here build on prior experiences that have provided the necessary knowledge base. The Year 6 students have already engaged with the novel through previous class work and their advance reading of the chapter. To supplement this, Maria feeds in more specialist vocabulary and essential background knowledge on an unfamiliar ritual. Similarly, the group activity in Isobel's lesson comes some way into a history topic. Students have already been taught some prerequisite knowledge and are given dedicated time in the lesson, before discussion begins, to digest some additional evidence.

Turning to the tasks themselves, research strongly suggests that a number of common features of small-group tasks are likely to be generative of productive talk for learning.[24] They include the following.

- *An appropriate level of complexity*: The task is within reach of the group, but there is an element of challenge.
- *A degree of ambiguity*: The task is somewhat open-ended and perhaps intriguing, without a single correct outcome or process.
- *A built-in requirement for collaboration*: The task relies on each student's contribution but does not foster outright competition.

- *A need to talk*: The task is engineered so that talk is not a by-product but integral, for example through a requirement for sharing different perspectives.
- *A shared understanding*: The task allows for a degree of autonomy but the broad parameters are clearly structured and shared.

There are excellent resources available, providing examples of activities for teachers[25] and, as pointed out by Rupert Wegerif,[26] once these activity conventions are understood as part of the classroom repertoire, they can be re-used flexibly across contexts and as discrete episodes in a variety of lesson types. Let's take a look at how Maria and Isobel's tasks show some of these characteristics.

Some of Maria's session is teacher-facilitated, but the SWOT analysis provides a focus for students' independent talk. The topic for discussion is characters' choices when faced with a dilemma so there is immediately an opening for differing views and the task format explicitly requires the group to avoid a single response and consider alternatives. While the analysis sheet also helps, as a shared object, to establish a common understanding of the task, Maria is careful to downplay the need for writing. *Talking* through the options is kept high profile. In the Year 9 history classroom, meanwhile, the activity is positioned from the outset as a debate about interpretations, immediately raising an expectation of considering different perspectives. The need to draw on evidence relating to the complexities of warfare adds a measure of challenge for the groups. The second phase of discussion, again without a requirement for a written record, adds a further element of ambiguity as the students are invited to speculate on an event (Hitler's assassination) that did not happen. Finally, the interesting issue of consensus is raised at the end of Isobel's extract. While agreement may not always be required in an open-ended task, the Thinking Together approach summarized in Box 11 below advocates striving for consensus as a way of stimulating the strongest possible reasoning in support of differing positions.

Box 11

Research in focus: 'Thinking Together'

Thinking Together[27] is an approach for teachers, presented in a range of carefully-designed lessons, which aims to create the conditions for the kind of exploratory talk mentioned above. Lessons are in three parts, comprising a teacher-led opening phase, establishing joint expectations about the kind of talk that will be valued; small-group discussions in which students talk largely independently and finally a plenary session to reflect on the talking that has taken place. The discussion activities centre on exploring controversial and ambiguous issues and encouraging the sharing of a range of perspectives.

A number of key principles underpin this form of learning, including the following.

- The collective creation of ground rules for talk, which can then be referred back to by teacher or students.

- Working in mixed groups which cut across gender, attainment level and friendships.
- Requiring groups to reach consensus so that sources of disagreement are explored in depth and strong reasoning is needed.
- The teacher's role as a model for exploratory ways of talking during whole-class phases, but remaining low-key during the small group work.

Thinking Together has been extensively evaluated in the UK and Mexico with learners between the ages of 6 and 14 and shown to have a positive impact on reasoning but also on formal assessments in curriculum areas such as English, mathematics and science.[28] The principles of this approach offer a useful model for teachers seeking to create both the classroom culture and the specific task structures for productive thinking through dialogue.

Closely associated with the structure inherent in the task itself is the way that both sets of students know *how* to talk. This is no accident, of course. We see in both excerpts further examples of some of the strategies introduced in Chapter 3, such as ground rules, talk detectives and sentence stems. Also apparent in Isobel's history lesson is the reference to talk roles, such as probing, challenging and summarizing and this is echoed in Maria's use of prompts for similar moves, some of which she then models herself. The identification and exemplification through printed resources of particular productive roles and their associated prompts or phrases is a form of developing the metacognitive awareness of spoken language that we have referred to previously.

In the 1970s, H.P. Grice famously proposed four principles for participating productively in conversations. He pinpointed, in essence, contributions that are informative, truthful, relevant and clear.[29] Analysis of conversations has also yielded a number of factors that help peers to establish and draw on what Mercer describes as making links between the given and the new as a way of establishing and drawing on a group's shared understanding.[30] Making the conversation flow in this purposeful way depends on moves such as referring to shared experiences, eliciting information and evaluating and reformulating others' contributions. The use by both teachers of identified conversational roles can be seen therefore as a student-friendly initiation into these principles by making explicit the implicit workings of discussion. Such devices are potentially very useful but it is important, of course, to recognize that they are one of many temporary scaffolds. Ideally, jobs such as Instigator, Builder or Prober will become dynamic roles that students will learn to move between fluidly in the course of a conversation, rather than fixed positions.

The composition of the groups themselves might also be considered. The optimum make-up of a group depends largely on the desired outcome. If the main aim is high-quality exploratory talk (as opposed to, say, the efficient solving of a problem) then, as mentioned in Box 11, a mixed group is likely to yield a more diverse range of perspectives. At this point, it is important to acknowledge possible concerns about the capacity of low-attaining students to collaborate with peers in this way. Adam's mathematics lesson earlier in this chapter, for example, was based on mixed-attainment working and a number of studies cited by Robyn Gillies suggest that low-attaining students may benefit a great deal from this sort of learning, if well-designed.[31] As for the number of participants, we see that when Maria's students talk independently, she splits them into groups of three. This is the number recommended in the Thinking Together materials as most likely to provoke reasoned dialogue without splitting into two equal sub-groups.[32] While Isobel's history students talk in fours, this reflects the different nature of the activity: unlike the need to establish a degree of consensus in the Year 6 SWOT task, the Year 9 history discussion is an open one, without a need for a single resolution.

In the analysis above, the focus is on the ways that Maria and Isobel set up their tasks to create the conditions for talk. Although the emphasis is on peer talk, it is possible to see how both teachers skilfully intervene at various points to keep the learning on track. In Maria's lesson, for example, the interaction has similarities to the approach known as Collaborative Reasoning,[33] in which teachers facilitate discussion around a dilemma within a text. Through her prompts, she is essentially inducting students into strategies for reasoning and challenging and then stepping back to allow them to argue more independently. In the next section, we explore this important question of the teacher's role in more depth.

Facilitating peer talk: the teacher as an active participant

The teacher's role in small-group discussion may take a variety of forms. In some types of activity, the teacher has a role centre-stage as a facilitating participant, as in the case of the Reciprocal Teaching approach,[34] in which the teacher explicitly models verbal comprehension strategies before gradually transferring responsibility to the group. In contrast, the teacher's role may often initially be less overt, with a focus on creating the conditions before discussion begins. Regardless of these starting positions, perhaps the most important function of the teacher is to respond contingently to the emerging interaction, as seen in the next two examples.

Classroom example: the teacher scaffolding small-group discussion
'Maybe you'll agree with some of what your group says and disagree with other parts. That's the kind of thinking you'll be using here. Now, what do you notice about this problem?' asks Suzy. With that, Year 3 children at Queensway get down to discussing the maths problems on the large sheet provided for each group. The use of counters as talk tokens helps to ensure that nobody dominates the discussion. This is mainly a discussion task for small groups, centred on missing numbers in subtraction problems, but the groups' discussions are scaffolded in two important and highly responsive ways by Suzy.

Firstly, there are frequent interjections, bringing the whole class back together in plenary mode to consider interesting ideas, which have the potential to move the learning on, that have been noticed through her eavesdropping. This involves inviting, valuing and supporting the sharing of specific contributions. Suzy's scaffolding role here, however, goes beyond the subject matter in question, as she also intervenes to support the discussion strategies themselves. At times, there is a direct suggestion made to a group: 'What would help here is to point to the part of the sheet you're talking about, like this: "If you look at Problem 1, then ..."' Secondly, there is also a form of metatalk operating, sometimes at small-group and sometimes at whole-class level. For example, at various points, Suzy stops the class and draws attention to good models of collaboration just noted:

'What did you just say to Ryan? Ah, so she's helping him to say his idea again, better.'

'Who was it in this group who invited Jess into the conversation? Yes, it was you. Gurdeep noticed Jess hadn't joined in yet.'

'What you did there was you agreed, but you also summarized what Megan said. That shows you tracked the discussion.'

Classroom example: bridging between small-groups and the whole class

At Eastland, students in Mark's Year 9 group are beginning to consider what changes they would like to see at their school. This is a project that will eventually culminate in a relatively formal speech, presented in front of an audience. However, the focus today is on collaboratively exploring the kinds of idea that might be worth pursuing.

The lesson features a frequent switching between small-group discussion and whole-group sharing. A progressive series of group activities has been planned, beginning with thinking about past experiences of change generally and moving onto discussing initial ideas for school-level change and then their own plans more specifically. Mark maintains a high pace through the lesson, partly through the variety of small-group discussions but also because each is broken into tightly timed phases, often no longer than a couple of minutes. Groups are given prompts to guide their collaboration. They include reminders on the board such as, 'Ask clarifying and probing questions' and 'Tell me more'. The discussion tasks themselves are highly structured and offer visual frameworks for categorizing ideas for school change including the evaluation of possible ideas for change using two axes to plot desirability and feasibility. All of this helps students to refine their thinking and keep talk focused and purposeful. 'Let's not waste time arguing for the same thing we've already got that's just a bit better,' suggests one group member.

At times, Mark leaves a phase of discussion mainly at small-group level, without a lengthy plenary, just inviting the wider sharing of an idea or two. Often this is prompted by overhearing conversations or by engaging with the group just prior to this plenary moment: 'Omar, I know you had a great idea over here – the one about times of the school day.' At other points in the lesson, Mark opens up the debate. Students are invited, for example, to suggest a connection between change, power and voice. Having briefly discussed this in groups, students are encouraged to share their thinking. 'You need power and voice to make change,' offers one. 'Even if you have power, you can't always make change,' replies another. Back in groups, another student builds on this, questioning whether they can ever really have power in school, due to their position compared to teachers, Mark steps in and asks, 'So can you be at the bottom of a hierarchy and still have some power?' This provocation reignites the debate and leads to another chain of exchanges.

In another phase of the lesson, Mark makes a connection between the familiar talk roles that students have just used within small-group dialogue and asks which might be most important as a tool for change. A debate ensues, with a strong argument being made for the role of Challenger: 'You can't develop other people's thinking without challenging or being challenged,' argues one student. As Mark manages these often passionate exchanges, he takes care to notice students who have not contributed and draws them in by name.

There has been a surge of interest in recent years in knowledge-based curricula in some Western education systems, allied with increasing attention paid to memorization as a measure of success (though it is interesting to note the contrasting efforts in highly-regarded East Asian systems to move beyond knowledge retention to promote a wider range of skills, such as inquiry and problem-solving).[35] A consequence of this is an emphasis on explicit instruction to reduce extraneous 'cognitive load' and scepticism about what has been called unguided, or minimally guided, instruction, equating this with pedagogical approaches such as inquiry among others.[36] Without delving fully into this debate, the examples in this chapter demonstrate how promoting inquiry and student ownership are in fact entirely compatible with structure and purpose when the talk is skilfully and subtly orchestrated by the teacher and scaffolds are in place to support working memory.

In addition to featuring other forms of structure previously encountered, such as talk tokens and discussion prompts, these extracts exemplify some forms of teacher intervention, as both Suzy and Mark interject in terms of both subject matter and ways of working. The most productive teacher moves in such situations are suggested by the work of Robyn Gillies in Box 12 below.

Box 12

The teacher's role in small-group dialogue

Robyn Gillies and colleagues have extensively researched the mechanisms of successful classroom dialogue.[37] More specifically, some of this research has focused on the role played by the teacher in facilitating such talk. Contrary to any notion of teachers being passive during students' peer discussions, Gillies argues for the critical importance of interaction that involves the teacher. Based on close analysis of transcripts of small-group discussions, Gillies and colleagues identify ten 'dialogic interactions' associated with better quality student explanations, questions and responses.

These interactions include:

- challenging students' understanding
- promoting metacognitive thinking
- confronting inconsistencies
- focusing students on pertinent issues
- posing tentative questions
- scaffolding connections.

Summing up the teacher's role in small-group Collaborative Reasoning[38] discussions, for example, Gillies points to three functions of these teacher interventions:

- *prompting* for reasons to support claims
- *modelling* how to present and use evidence
- *challenging* students with counter-arguments.

The case for the value of skilled teacher involvement in peer talk is strong, therefore. However, Gillies also emphasizes the need not only to train teachers in these strategies, but also to confront and change some teachers' personal beliefs about how children learn.

Relating to these 'dialogic interactions', we see Suzy intervening, for example, to focus the Year 3 group on the pertinent part of the task sheet and Mark confronting the possible inconsistencies in Year 9 around power and hierarchies in school. An important aspect of these interventions is that, while the issues might have been anticipated to a certain extent, the exact moves by the teachers are highly responsive and contingent on the emerging group discussion. This responsiveness to the learning is in turn possible because of the way that the focus on talk makes student thinking public and audible. Suzy and Mark can therefore eavesdrop strategically as they circulate among the groups and have a highly-tuned sense of when to let the conversation flow and when to interject.

Another of the insights in Box 12 is the value of teacher interventions to promote metacognitive thinking. Metacognition was introduced in Chapter 3 and the talk roles in Isobel's history lesson, in the previous section, were a useful device to promote this sort of awareness. In these two extracts, the teachers' commentaries on the learning illustrate another way of bringing metacognition to the fore. Suzy, for example, draws the attention of the group and sometimes the whole class to conversational moves she has observed from particular students. These include summarizing or reformulating others' contributions and inviting peers into the discussion. This signalling, again arising from her attentive eavesdropping, makes it clear that certain moves are likely to be particularly productive. In the Year 9 classroom, meanwhile, Mark discusses with his students the impact of various talk roles, leading one of them to reflect on the importance of challenging people's views if thinking is to move forwards.

A further point of note in both of these classrooms is the interplay between the small group and the whole class. Chapter 4 showed how paired or small-group talk allows for a rehearsal of ideas to bring to the wider forum but also important is the reciprocal benefit of whole-class, plenary moments feeding the group discussion. While Suzy listens out for teachable moments in the group task and responds flexibly by drawing particular ideas and collaborative practices to the attention of the rest of the class, Mark's lesson has a more explicit structure. His Year 9 teaching is split into a series of frequent, brief group discussions, interspersed with plenary discussions, which build the learning progressively from the general to the specific and with increasing levels of challenge. In this sense, we can think of the lesson structure as *episodic*. The idea of planning for learning as a series of brief, incremental episodes links to the approach taken in the various cognitive acceleration projects and materials developed by a team at King's College.[39] In their 'Let's Think' materials for primary schools, for example, small-group episodes are followed by whole-class discussion, which is a time for the 'sharing, sifting and refining of ideas' as well as bridging from specific group outcomes into wider forms of knowledge.[40] We can see this sharing, sifting and refining process in action as Mark both invites contributions from specific students and provokes debate about selected issues on the basis of what will move on the group thinking. A form of bridging is also evident as Mark links the idea of students having power to the more formal concept of hierarchies. One question we might reasonably ask is whether the sharing from small group to the whole class has benefits only for the immediate quality of discussion or whether it may have longer-lasting influence. Howe has recently investigated the impact of this sort of 'beyond group sharing' and reports cautious but promising impact on students' subsequent attainment in some forms of test.[41]

Drawing the elements together: a teacher's account

By way of concluding this chapter, the following example from a younger age group gives an insight into a teacher's thinking and her rationale behind a learning episode based on peer discussion.

Classroom example: stepping back and allowing space

Sam, a teacher at Queensway, reflects on a history lesson for Year 1 students part way into their study of Victorian life and the way this was set up to facilitate partner talk.

'I gave them an unlabelled picture of the inside of a chimney or of a tub and a dolly for washing. Partner A had one and Partner B had the other and they had to describe their object in detail so their partner could draw it. Then they had some labels and fed-in facts which they had to try and put onto the picture as a pair. That led to giving the pairs a pictorial map of a day in the life of a Victorian child doing a job like a chimney sweep or scullery maid. All they had was their knowledge from their discussion before so they had to talk to their partners about what they could see and what was going on. Then they had some more fed-in facts to go with the picture that allowed them to work out who the person was and what the job was. I kept stopping them at various points during the lesson to share a question that had come up and to see if anyone could help. At that stage, apart from posing those questions or repeating things I was hearing, I didn't say anything. At the end of the session, pairs from around the room stood up and presented to the others to explain what a day in the life for someone like a chimney sweep would have been. They'd totally worked it out themselves. I videoed them and the next afternoon showed the videos so they could choose one of the jobs to write about.

They were so interested and the learning stuck. You can even talk to them about it now. They owned that learning and when they were writing, they were using their words, not something off my PowerPoint. The vocabulary they didn't understand the day before, they'd worked through as a class so they'd really understood it and could write using it.'

Sam identifies listening as the main prerequisite skill for this lesson:

'One of the big impacts has been the focus on listening. In the past, Speaking and Listening was so focused on the speaking, what people were saying. We do a lot of groundwork on listening. It's not just sitting there looking and nodding your head. They are listening behaviours, but you need to be able to ask questions back and repeat things or build on what the person is saying. They are the skills that are probably the most vital to that lesson.'

Bearing in mind the age of these students, the level of autonomy they are given may seem surprising. However, within this account of what seems to have been productive and memorable learning are many of the factors we have explored in this chapter:

1 *Background knowledge upon which to base the talk*: Prior study of the Victorians, vocabulary, facts and pictorial map.

2 *Tasks deliberately 'engineered' to require collaboration*: A hidden object to describe and a degree of ambiguity in applying the facts to the picture.

3 *Prior understanding of how to collaborate*: Within the more general oracy work of the school, a specific focus on listening skills.

4 *Strategic teacher intervention*: Facts fed in at appropriate moments and pauses to share and clarify as a whole class.

5 *Progressive, episodic lesson structure*: A build-up of brief activities, including beyond-group sharing.

Chapter 6 will draw together many of the ideas from this and the previous chapter to examine the idea of a dialogic classroom in more depth.

Questions for reflection

- What are the prerequisite skills that your students would need to be taught in order to talk productively with their peers?
- What sort of tasks within your subject area or your commonly-taught topics might lend themselves to exploratory talk?
- What degree of structure in terms of student autonomy versus teacher intervention would be appropriate and comfortable for you and your learners?

Related resources

- The Thinking Together website includes downloadable resources for teachers: https://thinkingtogether.educ.cam.ac.uk/
- Oracy Cambridge have a set of discussion guidelines: https://oracycambridge.org/wp-content/uploads/2018/11/Discussion-guidelines-traffic-light-pebbles.pdf
- The Let's Think website provides resources to support the cognitive acceleration approach referred to in this chapter: https://www.letsthink.org.uk/
- The Reading Rockets website has Reciprocal Teaching details, resources and video: https://www.readingrockets.org/strategies/reciprocal_teaching

6 | Moving towards a dialogic classroom

Chapter preview

Truly valuing students' voices goes beyond individual lesson episodes to signify a deeper ethos underlying learning. Although the word 'dialogic' has already been used in passing, this chapter considers more specifically what is meant by a dialogic classroom. One of its key proponents, Robin Alexander, has noted for example that while oracy concerns talk, it does not *necessarily* presuppose a reciprocal interaction with a listener in the way that dialogue does.[1] This in turn raises the question of a distinction between the terms 'dialogue' and 'dialogic'. The chapter covers:

- Insights to frame the practice
- Creating a dialogic classroom culture
- Dialogue with a purpose
- Authentic student voices

Insights to frame the practice

The examples of talk practices in whole-class and small-group contexts seen in the previous chapters could be taken in isolation as specific strategies for an immediate purpose, or they could be indicative of a more ambitious move towards dialogic teaching. Dialogic teaching, often associated with Robin Alexander's work over the last two decades,[2] is characterized by pedagogies heavily based on spoken language which seek to develop co-constructed thought and understanding through high-quality discussion, reasoning and argumentation. As Alexander points out, however, dialogic teaching is 'as much a stance or outlook … as it is a pedagogical technique'.[3] Indeed, it is a stance with implications for how we view knowledge, power, voice and authority in the classroom.[4] While the ideals of the dialogic classroom align well with the 'participatory' argument for talk from Chapter 1, it is important to consider the practices underlying this ethos, as well as its potential impact on learning.

Alexander's vision of dialogic teaching has been refined over the years into a very comprehensive framework, including features of classroom culture and organization and student and teacher talk.[5] Central to this framework are six principles, detailing the context for, and content of, classroom talk: collective, supportive, reciprocal, deliberative, cumulative and purposeful. It is also clear, however, that dialogic teaching allows for a broad range of teacher and student talk, acknowledging, for example, that instruction and explanation have their place alongside argumentation and deliberation. This is in keeping with other research, showing how skilful teachers are able to switch between dialogic and more authoritative communicative styles, while maintaining a commitment to collective thinking.[6] Nevertheless, within this broad repertoire, certain teaching strategies have been found to promote higher-order dialogue from students. These strategies include: using provocative, open stimuli; allowing for lengthy contributions; refraining from interjecting too often; requiring students to build on one another's ideas; talking about talk and encouraging students to ask their own questions.[7] Alexander's version of dialogic teaching has similarities with a number of other models, including some encountered already, such as Accountable Talk and Collaborative Reasoning. Despite some differences in emphasis on, for example, classroom culture or the importance of specific talk practices,[8] common features of dialogic approaches include the creation of an appropriate classroom culture which, through talk, influences teaching goals and depends on a repertoire of dialogic moves such as extending, connecting and challenging.[9]

Dialogic teaching in these various guises has been found to have a positive impact not only on the quality of talk itself, but also on attainment. Some studies make these claims on the basis of correlations between types of naturally occurring talk and subsequent outcomes[10] while others report on formal, controlled trials of interventions.[11] What is also clear, however, is that dialogic teaching is likely often to involve a challenging culture shift for teachers and students alike, requiring a high degree of teacher confidence in subject matter and classroom relationships, as well as strong judgement about when to employ different pedagogical approaches for particular effect.

In this chapter's examples from practice, it is therefore important to consider:

- how a classroom culture conducive to dialogue is created
- the way in which different perspectives and voices are valued
- how teachers give students a measure of autonomy and ownership
- the way that time is found for inquiry and exploration of ideas.

Creating a dialogic classroom culture

A dialogic classroom begins with the creation of a dialogic culture. Alexander has suggested that teachers might usefully separate dialogic practice into two components: firstly, the *form and culture* of talk and then the *content* of talk.[12] By way of providing an intriguing contrast, the extracts to follow feature students from the near-extremes of the compulsory education age range. They allow a glimpse of the first of these two components: the classroom ethos underpinning dialogic practice.

Classroom example: creating the conditions for dialogue

In Steve's Year 1 class at Underwood, students are learning about sustainable development and considering the school's use of plastics. In terms of their interactions, they are also learning about the word 'building'. The word is displayed on screen, in a format resembling other 'new words' displayed around this vibrant classroom, with prompts to say the word and think about its meaning. Also on screen is a highlighted part of the cognitive strand of the Oracy Framework, signifying a focus this morning on content and ideas within talk.

Following Steve's lead, the children, sitting on the carpet, make a building motion with their fists, and it becomes clear why this word is going to be important today. Steve explains how this idea is going to help them to have a discussion and he gives them a sentence stem: 'I would like to build on Maisie's idea by saying ...' The children have just taken part in some whole-school activities related to sustainability and now this provides a rich stimulus for discussion. Steve sets up some provocative talking points using the format: 'The best thing about X was Y' and invites the children to agree or disagree. Initially, they vote with their thumbs, but Steve stops them and asks, 'Instead of just saying no, what could we be saying?' The children practise chorally saying, 'I disagree because'. Students then share their reasoned responses with a partner, while Steve joins the discussion in some pairs, sharing his own ideas in an authentic way and modelling the talk structure. At one point, Steve interjects when points become too one-sided and asks everyone to think of a counter-argument.

There is no shortage of vigorously expressed views on these close-to-home, authentic environmental issues. Debate eventually flows freely and there is evidence of talk guidelines, which are not referred to explicitly today but prominently displayed on the wall, being put into practice. They include things like: 'use a clear voice'; 'look at the person you are talking to'; 'take it in turns' and 'be a good listener'. As individual students then share ideas with the class, Steve invites new contributions, not as a disjointed series of ideas, but by asking questions like, 'Who would like to build on Ahmed's point?' As students around the room respond to one another, the clear articulation of ideas remains a focus of the feedback ('I like the way Dan restarted his sentence when he got a bit muddled') and particularly well-phrased contributions are noted and chorally repeated by the class. Having rehearsed their arguments in this manner, the children return to their seats and begin to record their thoughts in writing.

What we see here is firstly a physical environment in which the tools for talk are highly visible, from the explicit objectives based on the Oracy Framework to the prompts in the form of vocabulary and talk guidelines. The not-so-hidden curriculum message is clear: spoken language matters in this classroom. However, this is not talk that is technically proficient but devoid of substance. The subject matter under discussion is meaningful as the students are discussing aspects of recent developments and events relating to the school's commitment to sustainability and community action. There is a strong sense here that being able to articulate one's ideas clearly is linked to tangible outcomes. Indeed, as noted in Chapter 4, one of the motivations for Underwood's focus on talk is to enable even very young students to engage with complex issues that have implications for real action. Similar values are evident with much older students in this example from Eastland.

Classroom example: allowing space for diverse views in PSHE

Mark's Year 11 students at Eastland are learning about alcohol and drugs. As they enter, chairs are already set out in trios and warm-up talking points are already on the board. After some initial discussion, Mark asks the students to consider a photograph of a street scene showing police officers apparently dealing with intoxicated adults and asks, 'What are the red flags for the impact of alcohol or drug abuse?' As individual students select and explain examples, Mark gives a reminder about the body language associated with good listening. Without initially offering his own views, he invites others to contribute to each idea: 'What do you think? Same or different? Build on it.' The discussion then turns to what might influence one's decision-making on these issues and the trios rank seven factors including religious beliefs, friends and family. As they share, students are expected to justify their thinking and by now a more spontaneous form of building on one another's ideas is evident. Mark's role, in response, shifts from being at the centre of the conversation, eliciting contributions, to one based on drawing together and comparing the emerging ideas ('So Zahid's argument and Anna's argument seem to be polar opposites. Is that right?').

The seating plan now shifts to a 'traverse' layout with students sitting opposite one another in two parallel lines. Mark reads a story with scenarios involving teenagers encountering alcohol, drugs and peer pressure. At various points, he stops to allow the facing pairs to consider a particular dilemma. In doing so, they plot their thinking on an image of two axes representing influences from strong to weak and internal to external. After each discussion, one row shifts along so that new facing pairs are formed. During the paired dialogue and whole-group sharing, Mark eavesdrops and jots down notes. He supports students' language: 'So, Haleema, that's interesting. You say you "agree" with Sam, but you don't "agree agree". Could you perhaps say you agree but then use the word "however" to show a reservation?' He also draws attention to successful talk moves, such as asking an open question or prompting a partner to explain more fully. At all times, the emphasis is on students talking to their peers ('Say it to them. It's not me who's important') and there is a willingness to work with and follow a student's line of thinking in some depth.

Mark makes a final change of grouping. This time, students sit in groups of five with a designated chairperson and contributions are to be signalled by putting a thumb into the centre. It is clear that these various configurations and routines for talking are familiar and well-practised. The final stimulus involves considering how one of the characters in the previous scenario might have acted more supportively. Armed with the vocabulary, concepts and structures encountered already in the lesson, such as the various categories of influence, students are now in a position to talk and reason in a well-informed and much more independent way. As the chairperson in each group orchestrates the conversation, one student, Hiba, has been nominated to move around the room taking notes on the dialogue. By way of conclusion, Hiba shares examples of good talk practices, such as the sharing of diverse opinions and effective turn-taking. As Mark argues, students managing their own dialogue is significant:

'Good teaching is all about getting students talking and so I think lots of teachers won't find it alien to use language and to get students talking by prompting really deep thinking using sophisticated questioning. I think the leap is to teach students to do it to each other and that's the bit when the classroom becomes dialogic.'

These classrooms, so contrasting in age groups, nevertheless have clear underlying similarities as environments for learning. From the layout of furniture, the choice of activities and the values evident in comments, Mark's classroom is another with dialogic potential. It has been noted that dialogic classroom culture might encompass an orientation to knowledge (as co-constructed), an orientation to others (as valued participants in learning) and an orientation to the conditions conducive to the use of dialogue (through teachers' wider organization of learning).[13] These dimensions are all visible in the two examples here, but to focus in particular on the orientation to others, Alexander's three principles concerning the form and culture of dialogic teaching allow a further analysis.[14] A dialogic classroom, he suggests is:

- *Collective*: Joint learning is made explicit in Year 1 through the actions and repeated mention of building. In Year 11, the very same term is used, associated here with commenting on whether new contributions are the same as or different from others. In both classrooms, therefore, listening to and engaging with others are paramount.
- *Supportive*: These classrooms are safe spaces for sharing ideas without fear of ridicule. We see Steve, for example, drawing attention to a student's self-correction and Mark stepping in to help a student better articulate a qualified agreement with an idea.
- *Reciprocal*: The value of other perspectives is clear in Year 1 students' adoption of their peers' phrasing. In Year 11, the traverse activity format explicitly creates the opportunity to share with multiple partners.

Despite these indicators, this seems an appropriate moment to make a distinction between *dialogic* and *dialogue*. Catherine O'Connor and Sarah Michaels, for example, see the former as an ideological stance and the latter as a discourse structure. They also point out the futility of categorizing any single contribution, since its function makes sense only when seen in a wider context.[15] To take one example from Mark's classroom, his question about spotting the 'red flags' in the photograph shown could well be, if taken in isolation, a fairly closed attempt to elicit a correct answer. Instead, as the excerpt shows, it is the starting point for an open exploration of students' attitudes to a range of complex influences and dilemmas, this distinction recalling the discussion of authentic questions and uptake in Chapter 4. We might therefore say that not all dialogue is dialogic but equally that dialogic teaching is an approach using dialogue as only one of many forms of talk. This idea of a dialogic stance as an ethos relating to the function rather than the form of talk is taken up in Box 13 below.

BOX 13

Research in focus: a dialogic stance

Gordon Wells and Rebeca Arauz[16] have researched the principle of a *dialogic stance*, an idea later taken up by others, such as Maureen Boyd and William Markarian.[17] Both pairs of researchers have closely analysed episodes of classroom interaction to discern underlying features. As a result, they have proposed that it is the *function and purpose*, rather than the surface structure, of classroom talk that determines its dialogic credentials. In other words, no specific forms of talk should be either inherently privileged or avoided: it is all about how they are used within a broader learning context. Boyd and Markarian, for example, point to three indicators of dialogic practice:

1 Patterns of talk: are spaces for authentic student voices planned into lessons?
2 Agenda-setting: do students, at some level, have some control or 'interpretative authority' over the content?
3 Contingent practice: do teachers take up and work with students' ideas?

With this in mind, it is the teacher's work with the 'third move' in an exchange (as discussed in Chapter 4) that is all-important. Not only do teachers need to allow space for the sharing of views, they also need to commit to being attentive listeners who will thereby get to know their students much better.

Within these broad dialogic principles, there is legitimate scope for teachers to take a much more directive role at times. Reasons for episodes of teacher-led learning identified by Wells and Arauz include:

1 Establishing or imparting essential knowledge as a precursor to more inquiry-oriented activity.
2 Providing structure when students are unaccustomed to more open dialogue.
3 Ensuring that learning remains on track and purposeful.

On this final point, Wells and Arauz are careful to note that keeping 'control of the floor' in this way, does not necessarily mean keeping control of all the

> content: within a structured and progressive discussion, there is still room for
> student ownership of individual and collective contributions. Focusing on a
> *dialogic stance*, rather than on superficial dialogue forms, is a way for teach-
> ers to reconcile dialogic principles with everyday demands of the classroom
> and allows for a broad repertoire of talk types.

Boyd and Markarian's three indicators from Box 13 can be brought to bear on
Mark's Year 11 classroom. Firstly, students' authentic experiences and views are
at the heart of this learning episode; secondly, despite a highly structured lesson,
students are able to bring their own interpretations to the scenarios presented
and, towards the end, manage their own group discussions; finally, Mark spends
lots of his time working with students' emerging ideas, as seen in his drawing of
the group's attention to two apparently opposing views. Having established some
hallmarks of the culture underpinning dialogic teaching, it is time to consider the
content of that teaching and to investigate further the point made in Box 13 about
a place for teacher-led and perhaps monologic episodes within the dialogic whole.

Dialogue with a purpose

Teachers' decision-making about the use of a variety of talk types within an
overarching dialogic stance often centres on striking a balance between open,
democratic forms of interaction and the need for purposeful learning directed to
a specified goal. To reiterate a point made in Chapter 1, teacher-led, direct modes
of instruction are an important part of the overall mix, so purposeful dialogue
depends heavily on the use of teachers' professional judgement in drawing on a
rich and varied range of repertoires of interaction.[18] In the following examples,
two classrooms, both featuring Year 9 students but in contrasting schools and
curriculum subjects are juxtaposed. In these lessons, two teachers, Aleema and
Adam, work skilfully to ensure that dialogue is both purposeful and inclusive.

Classroom example: dialogue roles

Aleema's Year 9 history group at Northside is considering the lives of Victorian
factory workers based on a variety of sources and she begins with a
thought-provoking opener. Providing a quotation about workers' happiness and
the provocation, 'Is this really true?', she asks students to discuss their initial
views freely in pairs. Emphasizing the importance of evidence to underpin
historical arguments, Aleema then recaps Aristotle's conditions for happiness
and explains that students will be considering a number of sources as 'clues'
to evaluate against these criteria. They are to use a pre-prepared chart to
capture positive and negative points about each.

Firstly, however, there is some explicit modelling and rehearsal of the task itself and of discussion protocols. Today, the task includes designating roles within a trio. Using talk roles which are already displayed on the classroom wall, Aleema draws attention to three in particular. Taking one source of evidence, she adopts the role of Instigator herself and puts forward an initial, rather contentious, view. The room is temporarily divided in half: students are either Challengers or Probers and briefed on what these roles entail. After a few minutes' peer discussion in response to Aleema's opener, a volunteer offers in front of the class some probing questions, using structures like, 'What evidence do you have for ...?', 'What about ...?' and 'Are you sure that ...?' This questioning is rigorous and so Aleema initiates some debate around the boundary between probing and challenging, enabling another student to exemplify a challenge more explicitly. Students are given a moment to choose roles within their trios, there is a brief check for understanding of the task and the small group discussions begin in earnest. These roles, together with the use of tokens, as seen in previous examples, have had a big impact on inclusion across the school, as the oracy lead explains that: '[The roles] have worked really well in terms of making things inclusive, as you can see immediately which students are contributing or not.'

Classroom example: dialogue for inclusion

Year 9 students in Adam's mathematics class at Brookfield file into their lesson after lunch. The room they enter has tables set out in groups and signs on the wall reminding occupants that 'questions are important' and 'mistakes are proof that you're trying'.

An initial problem is posed on the board, presented intriguingly as an answer for which students must infer the preceding process. As discussion around tables begins, Adam reminds them, 'Talk about it on your table. It's important that if you don't fully understand, you discuss it.' Students talk through the problems, using personal mini whiteboards to work through and share their thinking with others. With a range of prior attainment around each table, some students, predictably, arrive at answers more quickly than others. However, there is a commitment to articulating reasoning and trying to ensure that the whole group has understood: students pause where necessary to backtrack and break down a procedure into simpler steps for peers. This emphasis is reinforced by Adam's prompts: 'If you're confident and someone's struggling, help them out.'

Adam's role during the group work is an active one. He visits tables to engage in dialogue at group level and offers some brief individual support for students struggling with basic concepts, thereby allowing them to re-join the group work. Where necessary, this involves the explicit explanation and modelling of specific procedures. At various intervals, he gathers the whole class and here his language, as answers are clarified, seems to emphasize the collective nature of today's work:

'Take one last minute to tidy up any last bits of the problem between you.'

'Kelly, tell us what you're thinking right now.'

'Did we all get the same answer on this table?'

'Do we all understand why?'

It becomes clear also that a degree of ambiguity is being deliberately cultivated through the choice of some of the problems and follow-up questioning. Adam's comments explicitly signal that he values the conversation and debate and at times, he intervenes to move the dialogue on: 'So, I'm now going to play devil's advocate and say, why can't it be ...?' With no written evidence generated and the interest in student reasoning, it is evident to all that the process is as important as the end product and that diverse approaches are valued: 'Talk me through your steps ... Well, that's interesting because I wouldn't have done it that way, but you worked it out well.'

As the lesson progresses and different tasks are introduced, the modes of interaction remain consistent. Whiteboards are still used as tools for shared reasoning and formal written work is not expected. Over time, the collaboration becomes more fluid, with students asking a neighbouring table for advice and one or two individuals visiting other groups to share their expertise. Only in the last 15 minutes of this double period does group dialogue cease. Books finally emerge, as Adam switches to a more instructional mode, explaining and modelling strategies for two example questions to be recorded by students for the purpose of future revision. As Adam explains the procedures, he voices his own decision-making, dilemmas and methods of checking.

At Brookfield, this use of a more dialogic approach is very much entwined with a commitment in mathematics to mixed attainment classes in this age group (11–14), as Adam explains:

'We've made a very conscious decision to transition to lots more discussion, open questioning and collaboration ... We took all the desks from being in rows and changed the arrangement so they could face one another and actually collaborate. I would never now go back to setting, purely for social justice. I wouldn't argue that this approach is going to revolutionize results for children at the lower end but what it does do is it gives them more of an opportunity to engage with the subject and enjoy their lessons ... There are greater benefits than the marks we're going to get on an assessment. We have far more enjoyment, which isn't one of the things that's measured, and far better engagement with the subject.'

To the three principles of the collective, supportive and reciprocal classroom discussed in the previous section, Alexander adds a further three which relate chiefly to the content of the talk generated, though of course there is a degree of overlap. *Purposeful* talk should be *deliberative* in nature, as contrasting perspectives are evaluated, but also *cumulative*. It is this idea of 'cumulation', or the building on others' ideas in a coherent way, which Alexander suggests is the most difficult principle to enact. In a curriculum context, such as the lessons here, it also includes bridging between students' understandings and the accepted knowledge in a discipline, while respecting the process of enquiry.[19]

To relate these ideas to Aleema and Adam's lessons, we can see that both teachers have chosen tasks and modes of interaction that are likely to foster both open dialogue and the use of reasoning and evidence in support of a position. In the history lesson, for example, the dialogue quickly moves beyond initial, uninformed ideas to a more rigorous, *deliberative* mode in which students not only draw on evidence from sources, but then have their ideas subject to scrutiny. Students' *purposeful* focus on the criteria in question is maintained by the use of a sorting chart as a shared visual object. In the mathematics classroom, meanwhile, the initial problem and Adam's subsequent prompts have an element of ambiguity by design. As noted in Chapter 5, such ambiguity means that there is a built-in need not only to talk, but to consider alternative views. The appeal to reasoning and evidence is reinforced by the explicit expectation that all members of the group and indeed the wider class must understand and be convinced of an answer. Adam's whole-class questioning pushes this even further: his use of 'Why can't it be …?' is a particularly powerful form of challenge. Also important in both classrooms is the provisional nature of the recording taking place. While formal recording can follow later, there is no writing in books during the dialogue phase. In different ways, the shared chart for sorting historical evidence and the temporary mathematical jottings on whiteboards are tools for articulating ideas but also enable 'messy', exploratory forms of collective thinking that are open to modification through a *cumulative* process.

The high expectations for supporting and challenging views respectfully, but rigorously, on the basis of sound argumentation and evidence, are similar to Accountable Talk, a form of dialogic practice outlined in Box 14.

Box 14

Research in focus: Accountable Talk and clear goals

In the US, an interest in dialogic practices is evident in the promotion of what Lauren Resnick and colleagues have termed 'Accountable Talk',[20] an approach articulating three standards for academically productive discussion:

- *Accountability to the community* concerns the valuing of others' views.
- *Accountability to knowledge* highlights a commitment to being factually correct.

- *Accountability to rigorous thinking, or reasoning*, is about the quality of justifications for claims made.

At a time when fact-checking and 'post-truth' have become high-profile ideas, Accountable Talk stands for the informed and reasoned sharing of views, rather than the unsubstantiated exchange of opinions.

While many of the norms and strategies for Accountable Talk mirror those encountered already in this book, a significant feature of planning for accountable talk is its emphasis on beginning with the *purposes* for talk. Surface features such as appropriate sentence structures and the semblance of linking to previous contributions are seductive but not necessarily indicative of high-quality learning. Three questions are suggested:[21]

1 What are my academic goals and how will the task I have chosen move them forward?
2 What are the advantages and limitations of the talk formats I could use in this lesson?
3 How can I best maximize the coherence of the lesson?

Learning *to* talk in a coherent, articulate way is an important part of oracy. However, an Accountable Talk perspective reminds us that a superficially impressive exchange, based on well-practised talk formats and routines, is not necessarily the end in itself. As with almost every aspect of practice, teacher judgement about the best means to a specified learning goal is essential.

As well as accountability to knowledge and thinking, it is significant that this model highlights accountability to the learning community. The value accorded to participation, mutual respect, but also risk-taking has echoes not only of a dialogic stance but also the coverage in Chapters 3 and 5 of ground rules and listening as a skill. The teacher has a skilled role to play in managing this collective effort. Indeed, large-scale analyses of dialogic classroom practice consistently draw attention to the way that student contributions are built on in coherent lines of enquiry.[22] Nystrand and colleagues have used the analogy of creating a fire, as:

- the *kindling* is set down in the creation of classroom culture and the initial provocation
- the *spark* emerges from the students' responses
- *ignition* occurs when open, free-flowing critical discourse begins.[23]

In Adam's classroom, we see the dialogic fire eventually burning brightly. Moving beyond small-group dialogue and a reliance on Adam's probing questions, the interaction becomes more organic as students begin to share ideas or seek clarification beyond their immediate neighbours.

Accountability to community also implies an inclusive form of dialogue. The comments from teachers at both schools attest to the way that this is at the forefront of their thinking. At Northside, the relatively formal device of talk roles helps to ensure participation. At Brookfield, a fundamental commitment to mixed-attainment mathematics teaching provides the rationale for the use of small-group discussions and reasoning in which understanding is to be articulated publicly and seen as a collective effort. The stances taken by these schools are significant as they offer a counter-narrative to any beliefs that participation in meaningful dialogue is only achievable for higher attaining learners. As touched on in Chapter 4, the work of Snell and Lefstein challenges teachers to move beyond such fixed views of student identity and ability, while acknowledging that dialogic practices are likely to amplify existing tensions between inclusive ideals and possible perceptions of some learners' capabilities for dialogue being limited.[24]

Accountable Talk's focus on purpose and academic goals as the driving force behind dialogue reinforces the idea of the exercise of professional judgement relating to varied repertoires of interaction. Despite the emphasis on dialogue in these lessons, they nevertheless also feature moments of teacher-led instruction. In the history lesson, the open dialogue in groups takes place only after Aleema has modelled one of the talk roles herself and explicitly discussed probing and challenging in a brief whole-class example of the kind of talk she is expecting in groups. For all the peer-to-peer talk of the mathematics class, we also see Adam intervening to offer individualized instruction to identified children. At the end of the lesson, he switches entirely to a different mode as he draws together the thinking into explicit explanation and modelling of strategies. As we saw in Box 13, there are a number of good reasons for teachers taking a more directive role.[25] For Aleema, it is chiefly about setting up the necessary structure for the dialogue to follow; for Adam, the regular summarizing of collective understanding and explanation of worked examples serve to establish the required knowledge not just for future assessments, but to underpin the next day's collaborative work. Such shifts in tone have been well-documented by Mortimer and Scott, as seen in Box 15.

Box 15

Research in focus: communicative approaches

Eduardo Mortimer and Philip Scott developed an influential analytical framework based on their close scrutiny of transcripts from teaching in secondary science classrooms in both Brazil and England.[26] Part of their framework focused on a teacher's 'communicative approach'. They analysed talk in lessons against two dimensions: dialogic to authoritative and interactive to non-interactive, thereby creating four possible approaches:

Figure 3 Communicative approaches

	INTERACTIVE	NON-INTERACTIVE
DIALOGIC	**A** Interactive / dialogic	**B** Non-interactive / dialogic
AUTHORITATIVE	**C** Interactive / authoritative	**D** Non-interactive / authoritative

While categories A and D are fairly straightforward, this analysis reminds us first that, perhaps counter-intuitively, B and C are also possible. Teaching can be both dialogic and non-interactive (the teacher presents different perspectives on an issue themselves and does not involve students or turn-taking) as well as, very frequently, authoritative and interactive (the teacher elicits students' responses but channels them towards a single point of 'correct' understanding).

The other reminder from this work is that a single lesson, or cycle of learning, will often need to involve different communicative approaches depending on the content and purpose of learning at different points in the process. At various times, for example, a teacher may need to:

- explore students' diverse views openly
- work with and refine students' responses
- bring the class back the accepted disciplinary understanding.

The dialogic teacher's role, therefore, is not necessarily to adhere rigidly to open-ended dialogue, but rather to use their judgement to make skilled, responsive *shifts* between communicative approaches, while maintaining an overall dialogic stance.

Using these categories of communicative approach, the bulk of both lessons might be seen to reflect approach A, with well-judged shifts into approach D. Towards the end of Adam's lesson, it is also possible to see hints of approach B, as he holds the floor but thinks aloud about alternative perspectives and strategies. Approach C is not particularly in evidence in these lessons but will be familiar from the superficially interactive but essentially monologic discussions converging on pre-determined knowledge, as seen in many IRF exchanges. The final section of this chapter brings together form and content of dialogic talk to address the question of authentic student voices.

Authentic student voices

One of the fundamental arguments made in Chapter 1 for a focus on classroom talk concerned participation. Beyond the persuasive cases that have been made for talk on the basis of collective learning, nurturing skills for employment, or simply effective collaboration,[27] there is the question of students' authentic involvement in their own education and ultimately their contribution to society. However, perceived challenges of letting go of both interaction and content, along with the way that engagement can all too easily be simply 'exuberant voiceless participation', were noted earlier.[28] With this in mind, school leaders at Downland explain a change of mindset for students and teacher.

School example: students 'talking back'

'All of a sudden, you have children who can argue with each other. All of a sudden, you have children who can question the teacher, in the sense they want to know more. They might not agree with you but they have the skills now to do that without being confrontational or rude. It's really powerful for children to be able to do that. I just wish we could teach adults the same! It's changing the mindset of the teachers too. Instead of shutting them down, which I probably would have done ten years ago, you can now have those conversations. It's teaching teachers that there is a place for children to be able to talk back: I don't mean talk back at you but talk back with you and question what you say to them. It's been a move, but we've got there. Now there is a real involvement of the children in their learning.'

'As the gaps [of spoken language proficiency on entry to school] have widened, we've been doing so much giving. Oracy is allowing us to step away from that a little bit to say, "Go and do it and try it, even if you can't write it, we'll film you talking it." Oracy has given them a voice where they can actually say, "I know this."'

As well as involvement, student voice in a dialogic classroom potentially has a 'political' dimension in terms of agency, empowerment and self.[29] The transformative power of a 'problem-posing education', rather than one solely based on depositing knowledge in learners was famously argued by Paulo Freire.[30] Freire recognized the implications for societal change made possible through a shift in classroom power dynamics and a different relationship between teacher and learner and indeed the following two schools see spoken language as one tool for making a difference both locally and globally.

School example: the right to be heard

Walking into Underwood, the visitor is immediately struck by vibrant displays and banners with slogans representing campaigns for civil rights, universal suffrage and sustainability. Evidently, this is a school where students have something to say.

In addition to the arguments for wider academic gains and life skills, Underwood has another reason for promoting student talk: a belief that children have a right to be heard and their voices can make a genuine difference. These beliefs are rooted in the UN Convention on the Rights of the Child which asserts, among other things, the right of children not only to express their thoughts and opinions, but also to have their views taken seriously. This is seen most vividly in the school's action on the UN's Sustainable Development Goals, which cover issues such as energy, education, poverty and climate action. Using their spoken language skills, students at Underwood have debated and responded to local issues and this has led to actual change. For example, they have agreed to ban single-use plastics in school, have lobbied school meal providers about food packaging and have undertaken a 'green the grey' project to enhance routes to school through the local neighbourhood.

Listening to learners: 'A voice to change the world'

At Fairway, oracy is part of a curriculum driven by the ambition for every student to have 'a voice to change the world', exploring who they are and how they connect with the world around them. Staff encourage students to go beyond short-term thinking about spoken language as a means to academic attainment and employment and challenge them to think about voice in a wider, participatory sense as future citizens of the world. As a school leader explains:

'We've specifically not called it Oracy. We've called it Voice because we think it's much wider than classroom practice ... It will allow you to consider who you are, what you believe and what your opinion is. What place do you want to take in the world? What do you want to change? What annoys you or makes you happy?'

In a dialogic sense, therefore, voice at Fairway is about empowerment, identity and impact in the wider world. Here, a Year 9 student shares his vision of being heard:

'Talk enables you to have your own interpretation of the world. We can't just be robots following an overlord. We're in a free society and we've got our liberty. The school always emphasizes we've got a voice to change the world. If we want to change the world, we need our own views and opinions ... When I'm older, I aspire to be part of the House of Commons, to keep on with what the school has taught me, like using relatability and humour. So, let's say I was going to introduce a bill, I could add more relatability and get more voters.'

By looking beyond the individual to a collective consideration of big issues, dialogue is being used in these schools partly as a tool for critical thought. As Wegerif argues, harnessing aspects of oracy such as collaborating, reasoning and listening as 'the vaccine against truth decay' is particularly important when considering the big issues of the day. These strategies help to build a critical awareness of possibly dubious information increasingly encountered online.[31] While it is often argued that much of critical thinking is domain specific,[32] there are well-established and well-researched dialogic approaches such as Collaborative Reasoning, which have been found to have positive impacts on students' reasoning skills as they internalize argumentative skills and communicative modes first encountered with peers.[33] Similar benefits are associated with Philosophy for Children (P4C), which involves students considering a provocative issue, suggesting questions, deciding on a particular line of enquiry to pursue as a group and finally reviewing the process and conclusions drawn.[34] Returning to this book's recurring theme of inclusion, guidance such as Voice 21's Oracy Benchmarks makes clear the need to value every voice in meaningful contexts *within* school[35] and these examples show how that ambition can also extend to the world beyond the school gates.

Questions for reflection

- To what extent is your classroom a collective, supportive and reciprocal environment for learning?
- Can you think of examples of when you make shifts of 'communicative approach' within a single lesson and what is the rationale in each case?
- To what extent do your students have genuine voice and agency for change within and beyond school?

Further reading and resources

- This UNESCO booklet provides a summary of Accountable Talk guidelines: http://www.ibe.unesco.org/sites/default/files/resources/29_accountable_talk_instructional_dialogue_that_builds_the_mind.pdf
- The British Council, in association with Voice 21, has a booklet summarizing discussion guidelines, talk roles and talk groupings: https://www.british-council.org/sites/default/files/its_good_to_talk.pdf
- Adam Lefstein and Julia Snell accompany their book *Better Than Best Practice* with a website of resources and guidance on dialogic pedagogies: http://dialogicpedagogy.com/
- The SAPERE charity's website offers guidance on Philosophy for Children: https://www.sapere.org.uk/

7 Talking with digital technology

Chapter preview

Chapters 3 to 6 considered the various ways in which talk can be both taught explicitly and harnessed as a vehicle for productive classroom learning. This chapter revisits some of these themes by exploring the role of digital technology. As well as being an everyday feature of learning in many classrooms (through the use, for example, of devices such as interactive whiteboards and tablets or features such as video or programmable applications), digital technology has some distinctive properties which can add value to talk. This chapter covers:

- Insights to frame the practice
- Providing a stimulus for learning
- Creating dialogic space through a range of perspectives
- Promoting metacognitive awareness of talk
- Adding value: summing up the contribution of digital technology to talk

Insights to frame the practice

As this chapter examines the role that technology might play in promoting purposeful classroom talk, it is helpful to begin with two key principles. The first is that it is almost always the wider stance relating to pedagogies for talk which shapes the way that technology is viewed and used, rather than technology itself driving the change.[1] The second is that, far from talk being marginalized by, for example, online learning, the principles underpinning good oracy practice and developed initially face-to-face actually provide the ideal grounding in interaction and critical thinking for an informed use of technology.[2]

With those principles in mind, there are a number of ways that technology has been harnessed in support of students' talk. A comprehensive review of research in the field found, for example, three forms of added value: the enhancement of dialogue activity; technological benefits associated with specific tools; and improvements to the learning environment through effects such as increased autonomy and motivation.[3] Examples of everyday enhancements to talk include the capability to adapt, change, record, revisit and share content flexibly[4] and the facilitation of small-group discussion in computer-based activities that break the typical IRF exchanges discussed in Chapter 4.[5] As well as these practical benefits, Wegerif is among those who have emphasized the potential of technology to open up a 'dialogic space',[6] involving students' exposure to, and engagement with, alternative viewpoints. These viewpoints might be gathered within a lesson through, for example, the joint creation, consideration and annotation of artefacts on an interactive whiteboard or other device.[7] Such artefacts have been described as 'improvable objects' which facilitate exploratory talk due to their provisional nature.[8] Peer-to-peer interaction can also be enhanced through online dialogue, allowing one group's ideas to be shared for discussion by another, using blogging tools, either within a single classroom or between schools at any distance.[9]

Technology use is not without its challenges, including a need for adequate technical skills, resources and understanding of adaptations to pedagogy.[10] The Covid-19 pandemic brought this into sharp focus as lessons all over the world were taught online. Technology-based adaptations require new forms of teacher development, but also foster new opportunities for sharing good practice by making time for professional collaboration.[11] Although research in the UK suggested that most teachers saw online learning as detrimental to students' oracy skills, there was also feedback suggesting that opportunities for talk through, for example, breakout rooms, were gradually being identified and put to good use.[12] Advice from Voice 21 highlights clear expectations through online talk guidelines and scaffolded interaction through chat functions and polls,[13] all of which reiterate the principle of technology use being driven by existing understanding of good practice for talk.

Providing a stimulus for learning

As seen in Chapter 5 and elsewhere, one factor in promoting productive talk is the choice of task. To the list of criteria such as ambiguity and challenge, might be added the need for motivation and purpose. While digital technology is just one of many types of stimuli, it does offer the potential for creating especially vivid learning environments, as the first two examples illustrate.

Classroom example: an immersive environment

There is a buzz of anticipation at Rushton as Sarah leads the Year 2 children into a darkened room. Once inside, they are surrounded by the sounds and images of the rainforest. This is the 'immersive classroom'.

Rainforest footage is projected not only onto three walls but also the floor, which is populated by scurrying ants. 'Where do you think we are and how do you know?' asks Sarah, as students turn to their partners to speculate and justify their claims. The setting provides an opportunity for factual questions related to the ongoing rainforest topic, but also opens up possibilities for using rich, descriptive language. 'Give your partner clues to something you can see here in the forest,' Sarah suggests, prompting children to describe in great detail specific trees or the dead leaves underfoot. Questions are posed to the children, including asking why there are brightly coloured animals in the rainforest. With abundant visual cues all around, students consider this in pairs before moving to a whole-class vote using buttons on the touch screen.

While this experience provokes a sense of wonder as a 'hook', Rushton staff describe the room as more than just a captivating gimmick. It is an opportunity to transport children, many of whom have rarely left the neighbourhood, to new environments which in turn provide new material, beyond their everyday experiences, to talk about. This room has also been a useful setting for more presentational forms of talk, such as weather forecasting: 'It's nice that they feel they are in the right zone, the right environment to talk,' says one teacher. 'It becomes almost like they are acting, they are so immersed, so they forget they're presenting to us,' agrees her colleague.

Classroom example: an intriguing film

Year 3 and 4 students at Downland have gathered in the school hall and are watching the short, animated film *Umbrella*.[14] The viewing experience is broken into three short excerpts, allowing for discussion at each stage. The film is silent and therefore especially intriguing, as there is a degree of uncertainty about the characters' actions. It is evident that this piece of video has been chosen in part for its ambiguous and intriguing plot, which offers plenty of scope for questions lending themselves to inference and a variety of interpretations. John's open questions as he pauses the film, such as 'What do we think is going on?', 'Why did ...?' and 'What did we find out about ...?', invite speculation and are very effective in provoking a variety of well-reasoned, contrasting ideas for small-group discussion. Reflecting on the process, John stresses the importance of choosing a good stimulus and explains the rationale behind the use of film:

'I find that children are particularly engaged by short films, particularly when they bring up interesting and relatable themes. Some, such as Umbrella, *do this brilliantly, lending themselves to open-ended and ambiguous discussion. Skills that we often associate with guided reading can be honed in this context: predicting, summarizing and inferring meaning.'*

In both of these classrooms, the technological stimulus has been chosen to provide a motivating purpose for talk, largely through presenting a visually captivating and intriguing scenario. In some respects, this could be seen as a variation on other non-digital resources, such as Talking Points[15] or Concept Cartoons,[16] both of which offer similarly thought-provoking and ambiguous stimuli. However, it can be argued that the use of technology adds some distinct additional value. For example, research on the uses of interactive whiteboards and student talk has suggested that their potential advantages for promoting talk include providing a large-scale focus of attention, the potential for multimodal learning and a degree of responsiveness, as teacher or students interact with what is on screen.[17]

Creating 'dialogic space' through a range of perspectives

In Chapter 6, the idea of a dialogic classroom was introduced. It was broadly characterized as involving a commitment to valuing multiple perspectives and, through sustained dialogue, co-constructing understanding among students. Digital technology can be particularly effective in creating both a reason for considering alternative views but also the means of sharing those views. In the following two classrooms, we see collaboration firstly within small groups but, in the second excerpt, scaled up to include sharing between groups.

Classroom example: problem-solving and teamwork on a computing project

Pairs of Year 10 students at Northside are in the computer suite scrutinizing circuit boards and components. A hum of discussion and focused activity is in the air. Their teacher, Ibrahim, has introduced a new element into their computing work: today's lesson involves linking their previous work on programming to the construction of circuits with outputs such as changing the colour of a bulb, taking the temperature and testing reaction times. Getting each output working is a complex undertaking, requiring following instructions, checking code, selecting components, combining equipment in a precise way and frequently troubleshooting for faults.

As the students assemble their components for each new project, there are inevitably many groups with unlit bulbs and silent buzzers as circuits initially fail to function correctly. However, this is all part of today's learning. Ibrahim has identified today's activities, with their many possible pitfalls, as powerful opportunities for discussion-based problem-solving and teamwork. 'If it doesn't work, I'm not going to tell you. You'll need to work it out together,' he reminds the students. Around the room, therefore, pairs of students talk collaboratively as they diagnose problems to get the circuits working and they interact in a variety of ways. Some students speculate aloud about possible issues: 'I think it might not be working because …', while others divide up the task and check their partner's work: 'I don't think that's in properly. Try this way.' In some pairings, one student takes the lead and offers a step-by-step narration of their process as they do so: 'We need the male and female connectors so I'm straightening them out first; now I'm getting started on this one …'

Ibrahim's primary role, meanwhile, is not to resolve problems directly, but to push the students further in their thinking, encouraging them, for example, to adapt the code to achieve particular effects. 'How could you increase the frequency of the readings?' he asks at one point. Some pairs work more quickly than others, encountering and solving issues that others will soon face. Ibrahim encourages those who have been successful to offer advice to other groups and, at one point, invites a student to address the whole class with a briefing on a particular strategy he and his partner have found helpful.

Building on the previous classroom extracts, it is possible firstly to see the role of technology once again as a form of motivating stimulus for dialogue. In this case, however, it also becomes an ongoing focus of activity. In essence, this is a small-group problem-solving task and, as such, has some of the hallmarks of tasks conducive to exploratory talk that we met in Chapter 5. They include an element of challenge and a reason to talk (the multitasking needed in this somewhat fiddly process). To consider once again the distinctive additional value of the technology, it is perhaps the way that it so directly provides the students with instant, automated feedback in the form of those unlit bulbs and silent buzzers. This in turn gives the students a degree of autonomy (since they are not reliant on the teacher to evaluate the success of their work) and provokes productive patterns of thought and talk, such as hypothesizing and reasoning, as they work through a troubleshooting process together.

In this classroom, students are encouraged to help other pairs but the interaction remains largely at small-group level. One way of opening up a wider shared space for thinking is through the use of blogging tools, as seen in the following lesson from Larchwell. This approach offers the potential firstly to expand the engagement with a range of voices and viewpoints, enhancing the scope for collective understanding and secondly to capture records of a group's thinking, allowing students to visualize and reflect on ideas at a metacognitive level.

Classroom example: evaluating arguments using microblogging

Sean's Year 7 lesson centres on a socio-scientific issue: evaluating the pros and cons of autonomous vehicles such as driverless cars. A microblogging application, allowing for short textual posts, provides an opportunity for small groups to engage with and discuss diverse perspectives on this issue from around the classroom.

'What do we know, or want to know, about autonomous vehicles?' asks Sean as an opener. Students in groups of three begin their discussion at tables, recording initial ideas on tablets. A few minutes later, students have posted a wide variety of questions which include speculation about the power sources and sensors used in these vehicles. Bringing the class together, Sean displays and organizes the posts at the front of the room for joint consideration. 'Using the expertise within your group, would you be able to answer any of these questions?' he asks. As small-group discussion resumes, he emphasizes that this is about establishing 'a shared level of understanding before we move on.'

Lively conversation returns to the tables. Reading the posts from around the room, students select and drag questions from a sidebar into the centre of the tablet screen, manipulating and sorting them into groups as they discuss each one in turn. While this episode is brief, the language is thoughtful and evaluative, featuring phrases such as, 'It depends on ...' and 'It could be ...' Maintaining the frequent alternation of dialogue at group and at class level, Sean now initiates a further whole-class discussion. He encourages students to engage with points raised elsewhere in the room and add their own views: 'Well, Rebecca's group said, "What are they?" and we think that an autonomous vehicle is a vehicle that doesn't need human help to guide itself around roads.'

Now that prior knowledge and early opinions have been explored, the lesson moves swiftly into a new, evaluative phase, initiated by the sharing of a video which feeds essential factual information into the burgeoning debate. Firstly, however, lesson objectives are shared. Today, they include a specific talk objective: 'To share ideas and information'. 'Where have we seen that before?' asks Sean. 'Yes, it's very closely related to our ground rules.' This is a reference to seven jointly agreed rules for talk, displayed at the outset of the lesson. With that, and informed now by additional material from the video, groups set about suggesting potential pros and cons of these vehicles. To begin with, ideas are shared at small-group level but, after five minutes or so, Sean once again guides the students to reflect on alternative contributions offered beyond their own group. Students are asked to split their screens in half and to select three advantages and three disadvantages. A constraint is imposed, however: only ideas from other groups may be used, thereby forcing students to consider a wider range of perspectives. After a few minutes' work in trios, the class reconvenes. 'So, I'm going to pick up on Taylor, Ben and Ryan for a moment,' says Sean, displaying the outcome of this group's sorting and inviting them to elaborate on their decision-making. As they do so, by arguing for potential advantages such as reduced journey times, they build on issues initially identified by peers in other groups.

Later, as the culmination of the lesson, students are asked to produce a written argument for or against autonomous vehicles. 'What have we used that organized our thoughts today?' asks Sean as a reminder. The immediate stimulus for the students' writing is therefore the record of the preceding debates and arguments that remains on the tablets as a legacy of the rich discussions in the earlier phases of the lesson.

Immediately apparent in this example is the way that the lesson and the role of technology are rooted in an already-established dialogic ethos. This is exemplified by ground rules, the students' familiarity with small-group discussions and a commitment to shared inquiry. While the blogging tool is not dictating the lesson approach, therefore, it does enhance it. At both initial exploration and later evaluation stages, students are engaging with emerging views from beyond their own groups, doing so both in small groups and at whole-class level. In this respect, Sean's role as the teacher is significant. He intervenes at frequent intervals to shift the frame of reference and provoke elaboration of what, on screen, are necessarily brief ideas. Also in evidence here is the value of the interface in offering not just a record of otherwise ephemeral discussions, but also the means of focusing on, manipulating and categorizing ideas as objects. In this way, students are able to reflect on and refine their thinking, developing new connections and lines of thought. These strategies have been more widely substantiated through recent research on the use of microblogging technology, as shown in Box 16.

Box 16

Research in focus: microblogging

Colleagues at the universities of Oslo and Cambridge have collaborated on a four-year study on the use of microblogging and its relation to dialogue.[18] Schools in Norway and England participated in the research, which captured interaction in lower secondary classrooms in subjects such as science and geography. Teachers were involved as co-researchers, implementing specifically designed lessons featuring a microblogging tool that allowed students to post brief contributions to a shared feed and then manipulate them on their group's own working space.

Analysis of classroom data, published in a number of papers, has yielded interesting insights. They include the way that such tools can help students respond to and enact a teacher's dialogic intentions for a lesson. This might be through, for example, the opportunity to browse a wide range of ideas and the way that initial contributions can be made in a tentative, provisional form, amenable to revision.[19]

More specifically, using a microblogging tool was found to be beneficial for:

- providing scaffolding for participation in whole-class discussion, by allowing rehearsal of ideas. Analysis of transcripts has found that spoken contributions to subsequent whole-class dialogues show a particular prevalence of talk involving elaboration and reasoning;
- promoting collective approaches to learning in which students see their contributions as part of a wider inquiry process;
- encouraging participation by quieter students, by drawing on the power of the collective effort to support in cases of individual struggle.[20]

Various platforms could be used for microblogging in this way and the one featured in this research is listed at the end of this chapter. While the research in this box focuses on within-class blogging, the technology does of course make possible similar and potentially fascinating dialogue between groups which are not 'co-located' (i.e. able also to speak face-to-face), but which are situated anywhere in the world.

Bringing together these two extracts suggests some further insights into other potential benefits of the technology:

1 *Dialogic space*: Dialogic space has been described as a potent shared space for learning which emerges when different, competing perspectives are juxtaposed and allowed to interact.[21] In the first example, we see productive exchanges of views but mainly between two participants and focused on tasks with largely pre-determined outcomes. In the second example, in addition to the task being more open-ended, there is a widening of the dialogic space. Just as a group approaches consensus, they are exposed through the microblogging to the thinking of the other groups in the room and the space is re-opened.

2 *Time to think and talk*: Classroom dialogue, whether at whole-class or small-group levels, usually involves students competing for the floor and bidding for a chance to contribute. In different ways, this competition is mitigated by the technology in these cases. In the computer suite at Northside, pairs work through problems at their own pace with automated feedback built into the task. At Larchwell, there is effectively a whole-class dialogue running throughout but for part of the time this is facilitated by the microblogging platform. This allows groups time to engage with wider ideas on a more intimate scale. In some ways, this phenomenon relates to the observations by Wegerif, Mercer and others of the potential for computers to introduce a gap in interaction between initiation and response: a question or problem is posed, a response is required but there is time and space for a *discussion* phase, thus shifting IRF to IRDF.[22]

3 *Provisionality*: As noted earlier in the book, exploratory talk is inherently provisional and can be facilitated by tasks and resources that allow for the

modification of ideas. While the first example here features mini projects with a specified endpoint, the troubleshooting required nevertheless implies a process of speculation and the refining of ideas. In the second classroom, it is not an artefact that is provisional, but each group's thoughts on the issue of autonomous vehicles. The microblogging platform, with its facility for not only capturing emerging thoughts but manipulating and sorting those of others, can be seen to act as a form of 'improvable object',[23] or modifiable, evolving record of students' dialogue. This idea of using technology to capture talk that would otherwise be lost is taken up more broadly in the next section.

Promoting metacognitive awareness of talk

Chapter 3 discussed the value of metatalk, or talking about talk, as part of building students' metacognitive awareness of their learning. Of course, a distinctive feature of talk compared with other evidence of learning is its ephemeral nature. While this is often helpful in promoting flexible thinking, freed from the constraints of writing, it can nevertheless present a challenge in terms of capturing speech as an object of shared focus and reflection. In this respect, technology offers a means of returning to spoken language for the purposes of evaluation or refinement as seen in these primary classrooms at Rushton and Queensway.

Classroom examples: audio recordings as a means to evaluating and refining talk

Working in pairs, Grace's Year 6 students at Rushton are hunched over information texts about World War Two bombing raids on England, looking out for and highlighting some of the specialist vocabulary such as 'invade' and 'bombard'. As it is a Wednesday, there is an oracy focus to the lesson and evidence of students' comprehension of the extract will be demonstrated through their collaborative recording of a spoken summary. As the school's reading lead explains, this is part of a move to reduce written work in reading lessons:

'The only time they record answers is on a Tuesday or Thursday. Monday is all about talking and picking the text apart, Wednesday we have oracy activities and on Friday there's a follow-up activity with no pressure for work in books.'

Having agreed their understanding of the text, pairs use a tablet to record their summaries, trying to score points for use of some of the vocabulary displayed on the board. Once captured, playing back the recording gives a valuable opportunity for analysis. While the focus today has been on reading comprehension and appropriate vocabulary use, Grace is keen to value other aspects of the performance, directing children to self- and peer-evaluate their speeches more broadly. The criteria for evaluation are familiar, as all children carry their personal planners which include a double page spread of oracy prompts.

Meanwhile, in Sonia's parallel Year 6 class across the hallway, the same technology is being used for a different purpose. Students in mathematics are working on multistep problems, in this case focusing on a complex question involving intervals on a number line. Throughout the collective consideration of the problem, there is an emphasis on articulating reasoning, as scaffolded whole-class discussion is punctuated with frequent paired talk. Sonia's prompts begin with 'Ask your partner how we might work this one out.' She then proceeds through reflection on the process, such as, 'Have we missed a step?' and 'Does that answer my question?' and concludes with, 'Now we've answered it, explain to your partner how we did it and the steps we went through.' This might have been a satisfying end-point, but there is one more move in this lesson.

Sonia recognizes that, of course, it is less solving this specific problem but rather the transferable aspects of the problem-solving process that are powerful. To this end, she asks students to use the notes they have made to produce an explanation for an identified audience: 'If I were to show this problem to a child in another class, how would they know how to work it out?' In the past, the audience for such recordings (often saved and tagged as evidence) has included the head teacher, providing a motivating purpose for the students' talk. Students begin to adapt their scrawled bullet points for personal use into more coherent notes for this summary for a peer and then set to work recording their thoughts on tablets, articulating their reasoning as they do so.

Classroom example: video recordings to develop awareness of talk

At Queensway, video is used to evaluate and share episodes of talk. The oracy lead identifies four overlapping practices, usually in the form of recording video using tablets within the classroom:

1 *Capturing evidence.* While school leaders accept that a focus on talk may mean less work in books, evidence can be gathered through film. QR codes are stuck into books so that they can be scanned and video footage of, for example, a science discussion in place of writing up an experiment can be viewed.
2 *Involving parents.* Parents had often asked what was meant by oracy, especially when there were communications home about events like a vocabulary dress-up day. Being able to share video clips of lesson activities has helped to develop their understanding.
3 *Linking to written work.* Sometimes a spoken activity is filmed and this supports writing afterwards; at other times a piece of writing, such as a

poem, can be filmed at draft stage, played back and revised as a step towards a performance. The final performance itself can then be filmed to add a sense of purpose to the whole process.

4 *Peer- and self-assessing talk*. Paired discussions can be filmed and then 'ladders' of criteria provided for subsequent analysis. Children then give one another feedback on their contributions.

In these extracts, we see both audio and video recordings used for a variety of purposes. Capturing talk in this way is contributing, sometimes simultaneously, to ends such as:

- accountability (gathering evidence)
- joint understanding (sharing oracy practices)
- support for writing (rehearsal of ideas)
- purpose and motivation for learning (providing a notional or actual audience).

In addition, there is a clear common thread across these classrooms of supporting metacognition in much the same way as we have seen in other examples through the use of specific feedback against oracy criteria.

In the examples here from Rushton and Queensway, the focus of metacognitive attention is mainly on aspects of presentational talk, or what Barnes referred to as 'final draft speech', refined and geared towards an audience.[24] However, recording more informal, 'exploratory' dialogue would be equally valuable and would allow a more considered version of the talk detective evaluation we have encountered previously. The use of audio and video technology to make talk explicit, visible and available for self- or peer-assessment in this way has a long history in foreign language teaching and has also been a frequent feature of teachers' professional development in the use of classroom talk.[25] In recent years, the greater availability in school of portable personal devices, such as tablets, increasingly puts this tool for learning in the hands of the students themselves.

Adding value: summing up the contribution of digital technology to talk

To paraphrase a point from the opening of the chapter, it is the pedagogy rather than the technology which is important. Nevertheless, the case has been made in this chapter for digital technology making a valuable contribution to promoting classroom talk. The potential benefits are summed up conveniently in the research review discussed in Box 17 below.

Box 17

Research in focus: a review of research on dialogue and technology

Louis Major and colleagues from the University of Cambridge published in 2018 a scoping review of research studies that linked dialogue, dialogic pedagogy and digital technology.[26] Reviewing key themes emerging from an eventual selection of 72 papers, the team set out to map potential enhancements to dialogue offered by digital technology as well as reported challenges for both students and teachers. Three potential and interconnected categories of benefit are suggested by this evidence-base:

1 *Dialogue activity*: Digital technology has potential for supporting productive forms of dialogue. Specifically, the review suggests that they are: exposure to alternative perspectives; knowledge co-construction; metacognitive learning and scaffolding peer understanding. To take the second of these as an example, a digital artefact or product may be shared and collaboratively developed as an object of discussion.

2 *Technological possibilities*: Nine ways in which technology provides distinctive possibilities for talk are identified. They include the opportunity to record and revisit ideas, to work on provisional, modifiable resources and wider opportunities for teachers and peers to evaluate and feed back on students' 'externalized' thinking. Perhaps most notably, the additional forms of communication and collaboration that are opened up can create a shared 'dialogic space' to share and explore different perspectives.

3 *Learning environment*: Research also demonstrates that digital technology can enhance the learning environment through the promotion of, among other things, greater engagement, motivation and inclusion. Work on a shared object, for example, can help to develop a positive classroom community but also, potentially, greater ownership and responsibility for learning.

Among the striking findings for teachers to consider here are the ways that digital technology is well aligned with themes from previous chapters, such as the power of provisional, ambiguous tasks and the importance of a metacognitive dimension to talk.

By way of illustrating these benefits, all three categories from Box 17 have been exemplified in this chapter:

1 *Dialogue activity*: The use of microblogging at Larchwell to open up dialogic space within a classroom.

2 *Technological possibilities*: The recording of talk at Rushton and Queensway to enable evaluating and refining.

3 *Learning environment*: The use of the immersive classroom at Rushton and the programmable circuits at Northside to provide a motivating context for talk.

Questions for reflection

* How might you use digital technology as an intriguing stimulus for talk?
* In what ways could digital technology enable dialogue between small groups in your lessons?
* Which occasions for talk would be especially valuable to capture, revisit and evaluate?

Related resources

* The Literacy Shed provides a wide range of themed video material useful as a stimulus for talk: https://www.literacyshed.com/
* Talkwall is a platform for microblogging that has been specifically developed for dialogic classroom practice: https://talkwall.uio.no/#/
* This blog from researchers at the University of Cambridge outlines some of the issues with dialogic practices online: https://www.bera.ac.uk/blog/the-challenge-of-researching-dialogic-interactions-in-digital-classroom-contexts
* Robin Alexander's video excerpts from lessons, categorized under talk types, are a resource for teacher or student analysis: http://robinalexander.org.uk/dialogic-teaching/video/

Sustaining classroom talk across the school

Insights to frame the practice

The preceding chapters presented strong arguments for promoting spoken language in classrooms, both as an end in itself – as a step towards being an effective communicator – and as a powerful tool for learning. Despite the strong evidence base, however, implementing initiatives successfully across a school brings challenges. These challenges are grounded in a number of factors, including the well-documented gap between the abstract world of educational research and the everyday world of the classroom[1] and the pressure of accountability, whether at local or national level, which can quite understandably lead to risk-averse school cultures.[2] The question, therefore, is how to overcome these issues and ensure that intentions really do lead to impact.

Looking at educational change at school level, Michael Fullan[3] emphasizes that during each of three phases – initiation, implementation and continuation – ownership of change and development of meaning at an individual level are paramount. David Hargreaves,[4] similarly, advocates 'collective autonomy', based on collective responsibility geared towards a common vision. In studies of professional development in high-performing education systems, this teacher-level buy-in is again emphasized, with opportunity but also *time* for collaboration seen to be particularly important.[5] These ideas relate to the Education Endowment Foundation's guidance on implementing evidence-based ideas in school. Their six recommendations make clear that implementation is a process centred on clearly defined outcomes, flexible and motivating leadership and ongoing collaborative approaches within the school.[6]

Turning to the introduction of talk-based initiatives more specifically, some common challenges have been identified. They include: ensuring productive talk in a whole-class setting, reconciling pedagogies based on dialogue with knowledge and curricular coverage and reframing the role of the teacher to allow space for students' voices and ideas.[7] Lessons from dialogic teaching projects point towards implementation strategies such as sustained cycles of development and review, in-house mentoring from expert colleagues (using video recordings, for example) and, above all, whole-school buy-in beginning with school leaders.[8] The many specific accounts on the Voice 21 website of schools' journeys towards introducing oracy bear out these principles, as well as emphasizing the need for common structures, a phased approach and an attempt to infuse talk into everyday practices, rather than seeing oracy as a discrete subject.[9] With a wealth of examples to follow, going beyond replicating others' practice in the form of short-term, superficial changes to observable behaviours is important too. Successful school-wide talk requires a sense of ownership and a genuine collective transformation in thinking. Indeed, it has been suggested that a deep understanding of the rationale for using talk on the part of teachers is a prerequisite for establishing practices which will really endure.[10] The hope is that this book may contribute to just such an understanding of others' practice!

Adopting a school-wide vision

The Oracy APPG report,[11] encountered earlier in this book, makes a number of recommendations for policymakers, but also for individual schools. They provide a useful starting point for considering whole-school implementation of talk-related strategies. Specifically, the report suggests that schools should:

- embed oracy across the curriculum
- appoint an oracy lead
- build a school-wide culture of oracy
- introduce shared expectations for oracy
- provide high-quality professional development in oracy
- ensure staff confidence in supporting oracy, particularly for struggling students.

What might be added to this list – since it is left implicit – is the need to take ownership of these strategies. This requires a clear sense of school-level identity that empowers teachers as autonomous decision-makers with a sound understanding of the principles underpinning the expectations of practice. The following example shows how one school offers principles not in a prescriptive way, but to guide decision-making.

School examples: principles to underpin talk

At Eastland, the analogy of the fire triangle representing the three essential conditions for fire is used to guide teachers' planning for talk. A model comprising three essential conditions for successful talk has been created:

- *Intentionality*: Talk has a clear learning purpose and is planned for and facilitated in a deliberate way.
- *Expectations*: The conditions are created through classroom culture, guidelines and teacher modelling.
- *Reflection*: There is a metacognitive element to lessons, as students and teachers explicitly discuss talk itself.

The model breaks down these three overarching principles into what the oracy lead describes as nine 'pillars' or 'building blocks', ensuring that clear and consistent language is used in feedback on oracy practices across the school. This structure helps teachers to make informed professional decisions about talk that take their planning beyond simply covering specific skills in isolation. It seeks to answer the question, 'How do we know that high-quality talk for learning is taking place?' In keeping with the fire analogy, the implication is that all three conditions must be in place if talk is to have purpose and be implemented successfully.

In a similar way, practice at Woodham is based on three shared principles to guide the approach to oracy: *purposeful* talk, *structured* talk *and scaffolded* talk. Purposeful talk links to learning and gives opportunities to deepen understanding; structured talk makes use of specific, well-chosen activities; scaffolded talk involves and challenges all children through the use of appropriate prompts.

The emphasis on principles rather than prescription aligns with the idea of building 'professional capital' and embracing teaching as a complex activity, as outlined in Box 18.

Box 18

Theory in focus: building professional capital

Chapter 1 raised the issue of 'cultural capital' and David Hargreaves and Michael Fullan also use the metaphor of capital. In this case, capital is used to distinguish between different approaches to teachers' professional development, as they contrast developing 'business capital' with 'professional capital'.[12]

A *business capital* view of teacher development sees teaching as technically simple and data driven. Strategies can be prescribed and implemented for short-term gains and teachers are largely interchangeable or even dispensable. In contrast to this training of individuals for quick returns, *professional capital* is about developing the workforce as a whole for longevity. This view acknowledges the complexity of teaching and emphasizes the cultivation of professional judgement over an extended period.

Professional capital relies on three other forms of capital:

1 *Human capital* is about the nurturing of individual talent.
2 *Social capital* enhances the individual by focusing on the strength of group interaction and peer learning.
3 *Decisional capital* values the kind of expertise, gained through practice, which allows the exercise of judgement in the face of uncertainty.

The development of professional capital, as the product of this trio, aims to create a workforce which is 'highly committed, thoroughly prepared, continuously developed, properly paid, well networked with each other to maximize their own improvement and able to make effective judgements using all their capabilities and experiences.'[13] The implication here is that schools need to think beyond the quick wins and uniform systems (important though they may be) and also empower teachers as collaborators, decision-makers and innovators.

By basing practice on shared principles, both Eastland and Woodham ensure a common, school-wide purpose and language for talk, while stopping short of prescribing how this should be enacted. Instead, teachers are empowered to apply the principles using their own judgement according to age phases, subjects and specific students. In this way, a more sustainable vision of developing talk practices, but also teachers as professionals, is conceivable. Focusing first on principles may also help to secure an understanding of the rationale behind the pedagogical shift that teachers are making. Based on their experiences of attempting to introduce more dialogic practices to secondary science teachers, Jonathan Osborne and colleagues, for example, conclude that such professional development has to begin with: 'first building an understanding for teachers in well-articulated and clear terms of the underlying theoretical rationale and the empirical evidence to justify the value of acquiring the new practice or practices.'[14] The extent of required exposure to theory and evidence may be debatable, but the underlying point is that maximizing the potential of classroom talk is about more than simply a change of skills and practices; it also involves an informed shift of stance and perspective. Beyond this, as discussed in Chapter 2, there may be a degree of trepidation around an increased use of classroom talk and this remains, for some, a leap of faith. Taking that leap, then, also requires a school vision in which risk and possible failure are accepted, as seen at Fairway in the following example.

School example: disrupting thinking

At Fairway, there has been a recognition of the need to *disrupt* teachers' and students' thinking and practices to a certain extent.

Academic attainment was high, and behaviour was good, so it was important to make a case for valuing other outcomes. In this case, those outcomes centred on giving students a voice and the potential to make a difference in the world. Even with a strong shared vision and buy-in for the 'why', the issue of 'how' remained. Teachers needed persuading to adapt their sometimes longstanding, successful practice and students needed to learn that lessons would require more of them than absorbing information (or the 'just tell me the answer' expectation). The response was to try and create an environment that allowed for risk and in which failure was acceptable, in contrast to the high stakes accountability cultures in some schools. The school prides itself on a supportive culture, through an open-door policy and peer-to-peer coaching but this has sometimes also involved challenging norms and assumptions by, for example, questioning whether silent classrooms are as highly functioning as they appear to be, given the school's aims around student voice.

'It does involve teachers taking risks ... We have teachers who have worked here for a long time and have got excellent results, so you are disrupting a highly functioning classroom – if a silent classroom is actually highly functioning. That's where we've had to be disruptive though and say, is silence always a good thing? How are students going to take their place in the college down the road if they've never been asked their opinion? Our students are already marginalized, so it's really important we give them that self-belief to speak up. But we recognize that's difficult for teachers who have a high-performing class in front of them who are biddable and doing exactly as they've been asked.'

As this example suggests, a vision for talk across the school is strongly bound up with school culture, so let's now take a look how schools have set out to embed this firmly in practices.

Creating a culture that values and gives status to talk

A common feature of many of the schools featured in this book is a culture of talk running from top to bottom through the school. As the head teacher at Woodham puts it: 'It's the schools that have been "all in" where it's flourished, where senior leadership has really bought into it. Some schools have wanted to do this, but if they haven't had support from senior leaders, it's just withered.'

Helpful in this respect is the alignment of talk with existing school priorities, allowing for clarity over the distinctive purposes that promoting oracy might have. For example, schools in this book have used talk to support other whole-school aims including developing:

- self-regulation and social and emotional skills
- functional skills for employability
- students as independent thinkers
- greater depth in writing.

Trust from school leaders can empower advocates for talk, but networks throughout the staff team are also important, as the oracy lead at Northside explains:

> I wouldn't be able to lead on this without my head teacher and chair of governors supporting it so vociferously, because they were able to talk at staff meetings and say, this is really interesting and really important work that we should embrace. That gave me a platform, as it wasn't just me asking them to do it. It's also important to include people in the strategic side of things, so I set up a working party, open to all staff. We meet once every half term to discuss where we are with our action plan and objectives, to ask whether there is something we want to build on, whether we need more CPD.

This effort to involve teachers at all levels and to ensure that talk is infused in daily inter-professional working is a way of building common commitment to the cause, or a sense of 'collective autonomy'. Collective autonomy involves shifting the focus from external to internal accountability or seeing one's main responsibility as being to immediate colleagues within a school-level initiative.[15] The following examples show schools using professional development and students themselves as models of oracy practices to build a degree of collective mission.

School example: students as advocates

At Southlea, as the focus on talk gradually moves beyond the early-adopting departments, students themselves are helping to spread the message about the value of talk. 'While we're doing things through teachers, I also want the students to be the ones to say this is something that's needed,' explains the oracy lead. To that end, open evening helpers are now trained in how to communicate as they welcome parents into each room and introduce the subject and teacher at greater length, 'rather than just saying "Business" and then standing in the corner because they have no confidence.' 'That's had an impact because staff in other subjects can see those kids coming in.' Another such outlet for showcasing talk has been the school's popular annual poetry slam, because 'the staff can see the impact that giving the students that voice has and that can be powerful'.

School example: professional development as a model for talk

School leaders at Fairway have avoided a uniform, top-down approach as the way into promoting talk. Instead, it has been introduced gradually through careful conversation opportunities and experiences. 'We've tried to drip-feed it a lot more, so it's been much more through discussion and collaboration because that's true to what we're trying to do,' they explain. For example, one staff meeting involved teachers reading in advance a range of articles and exploring them by sitting around a table engaging in a Harkness discussion (a form of inquiry into an issue based on sharing and valuing multiple perspectives and often involving diagrammatic tracking of participants' contributions to facilitate reflection on the process). This provided a powerful model: 'It addressed the *why* in terms of teachers understanding the impact on attainment and wellbeing, but equally they were also getting to understand *how* that sort of discussion works.' The hope was that, over time, this drip-feeding of experiences would pay off as teachers would internalize, understand and develop confidence in similar talk-based classroom strategies.

Building a culture for talk depends also on giving it high status. In the English context, a long line of policy recommendations over the decades from the Bullock Report of the 1970s[16] via the 2008 Bercow Report[17] and right up to the recent Oracy APPG report[18] have made this point powerfully. However, at school level, there is a question of how this high status might be explicitly *signalled*. Consider these three examples:

- Rushton has experimented with having no written work in its afternoon lessons. Teachers have therefore had the freedom to experiment with talk-based strategies, with examples of work captured and tagged electronically.
- Newton has had a debating week, initially devised as a re-launch of oracy as schools fully re-opened after the Covid-19 pandemic. Build-up activities through the week culminated in a formal debate between two Year 6 classes, which was streamed so that students across the school could watch.
- At Riverside, subject teams take it in turns to host an 'oracy takeover', each department targeting a particular year group and offering a week of talk-based activity. In RE, for example, students debate moral dilemmas; while in mathematics, groups discuss strategies for problem-solving and in drama lessons students produce a 'this is me' performance.

Much of this links to the points made in Chapter 3 about making oracy visible, offering diverse opportunities for speaking and expecting it to feature prominently across the curriculum. Returning to the earlier quotation about 'all in' leadership support, it is clear that some of the strategies involve a move away from written evidence of learning and therefore also a degree of trust.

The collective culture can extend beyond individual schools, of course. Like many schools, Downland has made connections locally through a hub and now around 25 schools regularly come together to discuss classroom talk practices and to share experiences of strategies they have trialled in their own settings. 'That model's been just amazing, especially for a relatively new way of teaching for us. It's been really powerful and a really nice way of bringing schools together,' says the oracy lead.

Building common understanding through modelling practice

In varying ways, schools have set out to establish common approaches to the use of talk. As the following example illustrates, talk practices are modelled at a whole-school level at Downland.

School example: using an oracy assembly as model for staff and students

It's Monday morning and around 60 Year 3 and 4 children enter Downland's school hall for their 'oracy assembly'. This is a fortnightly event and on alternate weeks their class teachers lead a similar process with the two separate groups. Although they are not leading today's assembly, these teachers will be participating along with their classes, as this is a valuable opportunity to see a senior colleague, John, in action. John will be modelling techniques and attitudes that can then be taken up and refined in their own lessons. There's a buzz of excitement as the children, mixed across year groups, settle down in a large circle. John begins by asking students to summarize some of the discussion guidelines that are displayed on a screen. Today's focus is 'agreeing and disagreeing politely', signalling that this will be a session about different viewpoints.

The initial stimulus is a picture, a still from an animated film, with the prompt, 'I see, I think, I wonder'. Children are quickly split into trios and a brief discussion of what the picture might represent ensues. Counting down slowly from 5 to allow time for conversations to be concluded in an orderly way, John draws together the circle as a whole group. 'Who would like to instigate our discussion?' he asks. It's clear that this is a familiar opening and lots of hands are raised. As each child speaks, they stand and take care to face the group. After sharing their idea, the speaker nominates another child by name to take up the discussion. 'Do you want to build on what she said?' asks John. This process is repeated three more times as children go on to watch short clips of a silent animated film. As the intriguing story unfolds, talk in the trios is lively and speculative, drawing on reasoning to back up the contrasting views shared. However, participation in front of the whole group is also expected. Different speakers initiate each round and some children without hands up are warmly invited in by John: 'I'd love to hear what you think.' Despite the large audience, there is no shortage of confident contributions today: a safe and supportive environment has been created, with a chance to rehearse ideas in the trios and an overt valuing of every voice.

While the bulk of the time is devoted to the children's discussions, John plays an active role in each plenary episode. Sometimes, he draws attention to the quality of response, in terms of delivery ('Wasn't Sadia's voice clear there?') or content ('I love the way you said you disagree with both those ideas. That shows you were really listening'). At other times, he probes for elaboration ('What evidence do you have for that?') or clarification of new vocabulary ('What does 'lifelong' mean?'). He also, however, plays an important role in modelling the desired ethos, making explicit his interest and curiosity in the subject matter ('I wonder where it's set?') and listening attentively and appreciatively to each contribution ('Thank you for introducing that new word to us').

The assembly concludes with oracy awards for students. They are nominated by their class teachers who have been looking out for achievements such as clear explanations and careful listening. As the two year groups file out after 45 minutes, the children take with them back to their classrooms new vocabulary, sentence structures and strategies for discussion. More importantly, perhaps, they and their teachers take with them a model of respectful and purposeful dialogue that has allowed for the collective exploration of ideas. As John puts it, 'It's so visual. It's there for everyone to see ... it becomes a snowball, with staff enjoying the sessions but learning from being a part of them as well.'

As an opener to the week, so many aspects of this assembly exemplify the sorts of practices and values discussed in previous chapters. Children's voices are valued and nurtured through rich opportunities for different types of talk. The fact that this has occurred in the context of an assembly is powerful because of the way it provides a model for later classroom-based work. For the students, the values associated with spoken communication have been brought to the fore through the discussion of the guidelines and the respect shown for their ideas in a highly supportive environment. They have had opportunities to hear their peers talk, both in the mixed-age small groups and in front of the whole cohort, and John has drawn their attention to features of speaking and listening considered effective. Over time, these fortnightly assemblies create a shared framework for the school: a way of communicating, but also a way of thinking and behaving more broadly. For the class teachers, their attendance is significant, as this is a model for them too. Seeing colleagues teach is a rarity in many schools. Here, they have seen John demonstrate such things as:

• choosing a stimulus for talk
• organizing and grouping children

- agreeing ground rules
- providing varied opportunities for talk
- handling responses in a cumulative way
- drawing out teaching points related to talk
- actively scaffolding talk structures.

Above all, John has exemplified this practice in his own speech and interactions as part of a collective community of inquiry. This use of modelling to show classroom talk in practice can also be distributed among a small number of 'early adopters', as seen in the following examples.

School examples: early adopters as 'pioneers' and 'champions'

At Rushton, the oracy lead and one other colleague spent a term trying out strategies in English and mathematics contexts respectively. Coming from their positions in different year groups and with these different subject experiences, they were then able to come to the wider staff team with a convincing 'double pronged approach'. Subsequently, this school has designated an 'oracy champion' in each key stage, so that advice is always readily available. Similarly, at Queensway, a central oracy team with one representative from each year group, tries out new ideas first and then disseminates to their colleagues. In a secondary context, Fairway School worked out who might be excited about oracy and, with a little coaxing, managed to ensure coverage across each faculty. This was seen to be important so that the messages about talk were not exclusively associated with one person from a particular disciplinary background. As a school leader put it, 'It absolutely had to be me talking to the subject experts and them guiding the conversation.' At Southlea, meanwhile, an initial group from English, history and geography had begun the process by trying out strategies. These teachers were then gradually sharing their expertise by, in turn, nurturing similar 'pioneers' emerging in other departments, as the oracy lead explains:

'Now we've got this thing where people from those departments just pop into each other's classrooms when there are talk tasks going on so they can view it. It's that idea too that word of mouth is important ... I'm using [the pioneers] as my resource. The idea is that they are experts who other people can go to and work with. So they are the experts and I just provide them with support if they need it. Unlike normal CPD which often seems fabulous but doesn't work when you try and put it into practice, when you've got people actually doing it, it's very easy just to go and see that person.'

Linking to the idea of professional capital, these examples from diverse schools all acknowledge the power of fellow teachers' testimony for building trust in new practices but also show the respect accorded to existing expertise held in particular age phases or subjects. The use of school colleagues as 'champions' or 'pioneers' to trial, model and support new talk-related practices relates to well-established distributed forms of professional development. Research projects introducing dialogic practices have frequently made use of similar 'ambassadors', 'instructional leaders' or 'mentors' at school level.[19] As well as making professional development sustainable, this approach also allows a degree of autonomy when compared with a strictly top-down implementation, as teachers can collaborate and innovate in what is itself a dialogic process with what has been termed 'guided agency'.[20]

Supporting talk through school-wide structures and resources

Despite the importance of maintaining teacher ownership and a degree of autonomy, supporting teachers with an oracy curriculum or curated resources is another form of developing a shared understanding. A further motivation is also to make the incorporation of talk as straightforward as possible, minimizing teachers' workloads by collating banks of resources or even producing physical or digital materials that are ready to use and adapt.

School example: Voice lessons providing a foundation

Voice is one of five themes at Fairway (others include performing arts and citizenship) which are taught on rotation to Years 7 and 8. The focus in Year 7 is on familiarization with the Oracy Framework and developing balanced arguments on themes such as deforestation, toxic masculinity and fake news. In Year 8, attention shifts to presentational aspects of talk, culminating in performances of spoken word poetry focused on celebrating students' identities and authentic dialects. While this in some ways represents a discrete oracy curriculum for these year groups, the idea is that these are skills to be honed in this environment, but then applied across the curriculum. As the teacher leading this explains, 'They might practise sentence stems with me on Monday morning in a voice lesson but the expectation is that they then use them in history that afternoon, or in science the following morning.'

Beginning with these voice lessons, therefore, students' skills and associated resources for the staff are primed for feeding into lessons across the school to be built upon and applied in different curricular contexts. The introduction of 'Talk Tuesdays' when teachers are encouraged to develop their practice and try out talk-based activities, supported by a booklet of generic activity ideas, is another way of facilitating this dissemination of practice.

School example: an oracy toolkit for teachers

At Woodham, based on teachers' ideas, an oracy 'toolkit' has been created as a way of capturing some of the talk strategies that might be employed. The toolkit document offers a range of activity types, such as odd one out, ranking and hot seating. Each activity is accompanied by an explanation of its use, complete with visual examples of resources, and suggestions for contexts across the curriculum in which it might be especially beneficial. In a related resource, the same activities have been helpfully categorized for teachers under types of talk structure (such as reasoning, reflecting, linking, comparing) together with examples of related questions. Aligned to this, resources such as sentence stems and picture prompts have been created along with the school's own version of discussion roles within groups. 'When we first introduced the toolkit,' says the oracy lead, 'we gave each year group a challenge: "Let's all try something different and next week share what we tried." And then the next week we tried something different that no one had tried and then shared that the following week. We kept it positive so we were all experimenting together and trying things at the same time.'

In their different ways, these examples show common skills, teaching strategies and resources infusing the curriculum. While this might initially seem at odds with teachers' own judgement, the justification for these shared systems is made persuasively by Michaels and her colleagues behind Accountable Talk.[21] Consistent with the current interest in supporting working memory, they argue that a stable framework of recurring, predictable routines frees up students to think about the substantive content of a lesson rather than the mechanisms of interaction. Also emphasized is the idea that, while routines may be standard, their deployment at particular times depends on teacher judgement about learning goals: 'Academic goals and purposes, not just sociability, must drive the talk. The routine nature of the event simply creates the structural supports for high levels of thinking and participation by all students.'[22] Once a shared understanding of talk principles and practices is established, a further consideration is the monitoring of their progression through the school and this is the subject of the next section.

Ensuring progression in talk through the school

While informal student self- and peer-assessment is part of the metacognitive awareness of talk, assessing student talk and ensuring progression through the school is for many schools a work in progress. The purposes of, and inferences drawn from, assessment may be formative or summative in character[23] but they nevertheless rely on agreed criteria for success and some means of the student demonstrating those criteria. While preceding chapters have shown similarities in teaching strategies across settings, the head teacher at Underwood highlights the difficulty of coming to a single view on assessment:

> *Assessment is the hardest challenge. You want to have the ability to assess accurately what your progression of learning looks like but progression in a school in a diverse community in [city] will be very different from a Home Counties school where everyone has English as their first language. There are different challenges for different schools.*

The lack of consensus relates partly to an inherent tension. On the one hand, a robust process for assessment helps to give talk greater status. While spoken language has been marginalized in English statutory assessment, in France, for example, 'Le Grand Oral', a formal spoken presentation, is a central part of recent reforms to the school-leavers' *baccalauréat*.[24] On the other hand, however, there are fears that formalizing assessment in what Alexander has called 'ill-conceived tests' risks narrowing and distorting the range of talk that is valued.[25] Not only this, but there is the challenge alluded to in previous chapters of agreeing on criteria, or even broad conventions, for successful speech for a multitude of purposes and contexts.

Nevertheless, partly in response to a stated need to give 'attention' to talk, Mercer and colleagues at Cambridge developed and tested an oracy assessment toolkit.[26] Although the toolkit was initially focused on Year 7 students, it included the development of the Oracy Framework referred to in previous chapters. This framework has been used as a starting point for some schools' own assessment and progression processes in a variety of ways.

School examples: Progression based on the Oracy Framework

At Queensway, a whole-school progression document underpins oracy assessment. The oracy lead explains how this evolved from local collaboration:

'A development group for leads of speaking and listening was created. At the time, the new curriculum had just come out and speaking and listening was just tiny and we said, we can't cope with this. So we pooled all the resources we'd got and created an assessment framework from age four to eleven. Then we created exemplification and video materials to go alongside it. All the schools in our group had this material. People ran with it and it became used in the city but the document was massive, A4 sheets with 'I can' statements from top to bottom. So, as

good as it was, it still wasn't incredibly workable. From there, we continued to work together and meet once a term and it pushed everything forward.'

More recent developments, now influenced by involvement with Voice 21 have seen the emergence of a more concise document. This is broken into four age phases, showing expectations against each of the four strands of the Oracy Framework and is used to guide the tracking of three sample students through the year.

'It's taken a long time to compile but we've tried to link it to the four areas of the Framework. It's a lovely document and progresses from early years all the way to Year 6 and just shows you what the expected progression in discussion, for example, would be.'

Staff at Rushton also log progress against the four framework strands, though 'reorganized to what we felt fit best for us,' and do so largely based on teacher observation and using an online application. This means that evidence, such as recordings of talk, can be tagged and colour coded according to competence levels. As one staff member explains: 'Having the [technology] alongside oracy is huge. If we didn't have it, it would be very difficult for us to see just how well they are progressing with their talking.'

In contrast, however, a school leader at Downland explains the decision not to introduce formal assessment:

'We don't assess oracy in any formalized way because we feel that would detract from practice and you end up with teaching to certain criteria, which isn't necessarily helpful. We all use the Framework though. We set targets against the four elements so, in that sense, there is assessment going on but we don't break it down term by term. I'm not sure it's helpful to do so as it wouldn't enrich anything. However, I completely buy the argument that until there's more acknowledgement of oracy in the National Curriculum and probably in some sort of formalized testing, you're going to struggle to get the buy-in across the board.'

In addition to the challenge of agreeing a universal set of criteria, these examples illustrate some of the dilemmas of implementation. Queensway and Rushton have gradually developed more manageable approaches but Downland's stance highlights the fear of constraint and a loss of authenticity. Other challenges of assessing talk include its fleeting nature, the difficulty of assessing multiple students without making a recording, the need to understand the wider context of any contribution and the difficulty of isolating a single student within a group dialogue.[27] The following example from Woodham shows one teacher's response to some of these issues, as tracking against the Oracy Framework is supplemented by an additional approach.

School example: delving deeper

At Woodham, there is a whole-school approach to monitoring oracy progress. This is based in part on a progression document of 'I can' statements for each year group, breaking down skills under headings which partly echo the Oracy Framework strands: presenting, language, content and audience. Teachers use this as a prompt for planning and then plot students' achievements on a grid which captures both skills and contribution levels. This has formative value at individual class level, enabling teachers to spot areas for development. In order to track progress across the school, Voice 21's Oracy Benchmarks (see Chapter 2) have been adapted for this school's specific context and linked to a five-point scoring system. Individual teachers data feed into a whole-class analysis each term which allows the oracy lead to spot patterns at a higher level.

To complement this comprehensive, yet necessarily surface-level, tracking of skills, Amy, Woodham's oracy lead, has trialled an additional form of assessment. This involved recording and then looking very closely at a single group's independent interaction during a task. As she explains:

'It was about delving a bit deeper, because on the surface everything looked absolutely fine: their presentational talk was great and oracy assemblies were going well. It was only when I was listening into children's discussions that I realized there were some children sitting doing nothing, others talking over each other. It was only when listening closely that I noticed the issues, but on the surface you wouldn't have thought so.'

Amy used a coding system developed by the University of Cambridge (see Box 19 below) to classify students' contributions in categories such as inviting reasoning or building on others' ideas. She chose a group who seemed not to use talk as effectively as others in an attempt to uncover how they interacted when talking about a task unsupervised with their peers. The detailed analysis of this talk had long-lasting effects on her practice beyond this particular 'sample' group.

'I can still hear them do it now and I think it's helped me as a teacher who plans for opportunities for oracy to really think about what kind of talk my children are going to get from this activity. What do I want them to do? It's helped me plan for helping children to keep conversations going. It's made me think about how they can manage their own discussions. Since doing that, it's helped me develop our discussion roles further. The role of the motivator in particular: recognizing good ideas and inviting other people to join.'

The value of setting out to capture and notice 'spontaneous' and informal task-related talk through a recording rather than overt participation with the group had been particularly important:

'Children are on best behaviour when they're giving that presentational talk to the teacher or sharing an answer in front of everybody. It's when they're talking with their group or partner that they let their guard down and they weren't giving the same quality of talk. I got quite a good insight into how it must be and what their experiences are when I say, 'talk to a partner'. Even just from looking at that small group, I realized that everyone needed that training on how to be a good talk partner. It's not something I'd ever noticed because if you're there with a group, they put on a front.'

While Amy uses the Oracy Framework as the basis for monitoring progression across the school, she therefore recognizes the danger of reducing the richness of classroom talk to a series of skills to be ticked off. The materials mentioned in Box 19 offer an additional, complementary perspective. They make possible not an individual grading of a skill, but a more holistic evaluation of educationally productive dialogue in a more natural context, in line with the hallmarks of exploratory talk from Chapter 5, for example.

Box 19

Research in focus: coding classroom talk as a means of evaluation

One approach to evaluating classroom talk is to look closely at examples of interaction and categorize the talk going on. This allows teachers to identify the prevalence of, but also the conditions for, productive dialogue.

Teams from the University of Cambridge and the National Autonomous University of Mexico have developed a coding scheme for the analysis of the form and function of both peer and student–teacher dialogue in the classroom.[28] The Scheme for Educational Dialogue Analysis (SEDA) is the result of a rigorous, iterative process of identifying and progressively clustering features of talk into a small number of categories at the level of individual communicative acts, or utterances, which arise from broader communicative events and communicative situations. Categories of dialogue, each with a code, a description and vocabulary likely to be heard include:

- building
- challenging
- reasoning
- connecting
- reflecting on dialogue
- inviting ideas.

While initially developed for educational researchers, SEDA is designed to be adapted freely. One such adaptation, T-SEDA, is a version for use by teachers for inquiry into their own classroom practice.[29] T SEDA is a comprehensive resource comprising not only descriptions and examples of 10 categories of talk, but a wealth of materials such as video exemplification, coding templates and guidance on practitioner inquiry more generally. All of this is housed on a website specifically designed for teachers.

From Amy's account we see that, while the process offered insight into this particular group, she did not feel the need to replicate this with all the students in her classroom. What she had effectively done was to capture an example from one group against which she could use as a benchmark for thinking about her class as a whole. The principle of assessing through establishing benchmark examples relates to another approach to the assessment of talk which has been suggested as a possible way forward. Comparative judgement sidesteps some of the problems involved with subjective assessments by requiring teachers to compare multiple different pairs of example 'performances' (in this case, video footage of students talking), with a view to producing a reliable ranking[30] and this may prove to be a viable way forward. The final theme in this chapter takes us beyond the classroom, out of the school gates and into the homes of the students.

Involving families in developing spoken language

As shown throughout this book, valuing, harnessing and teaching spoken language is more than just a classroom strategy or a part of the curriculum. It is often a broad ethos based on aspirations for students' lifelong prospects. As such, it is natural that schools should want effective talk to extend beyond the classroom. Indeed, many schools invite families to witness the talk going in contexts such as oracy assemblies at Downlands and poetry readings at Woodham. At Eastland, the annual, high-profile event involving students' presentations about community issues took place online during the 2020–21 pandemic and, for one tutor group, families were invited to join each student and to participate by offering feedback. At Northside, meanwhile, this family involvement has been extended to a structured approach to parents' evening conversations, as seen in the following example.

School example: bringing oracy skills into parents' evenings

Northside's oracy lead explains why parents' evenings have been identified as an opportunity to raise both awareness and the status of spoken language: *'I was motivated by the idea of engaging parents more. We'd talked to them about oracy through newsletters and coffee mornings but hadn't really had any questions or interest back about what that meant or what it was.'*

Every Year 7 student is asked in advance of the event to pick a piece of work that they are proud of, which is then displayed on boards across the school hall. Students stand by their work and parents are given a feedback form prompting them to ask their child to explain the work. The feedback forms specifically ask for feedback on aspects of spoken communication. As well as initiating conversations with teachers about the subject, as the adults begin to comment on things like eye contact and clarity of speech, the process helps to build an understanding of oracy: *'It's difficult for parents to understand the importance [of oracy] if the child is doing well. It helped our parents to see that it's not just about results and we have had a lot more parental engagement because of that.'*

In particular, this sort of interaction seems to build bridges with parents who speak little or no English at home, as it gives status to the wider linguistic assets that families bring with them into the school:

'It allowed us to talk about other aspects of oracy which, in some ways, are even more important: the physical gestures, the fact you need to earnestly think about what you talk about and demonstrate that in the way that you speak. A lot of parents liked that. They thought, I can do that at home with my child and have those conversations.'

Beyond showcasing events in school, however, schools have also sought to promote talk within families, capitalizing on the home environment. This is a recognition of the point made in Chapter 1 about households' 'funds of knowledge' that can be valued and tapped into,[31] as seen in the following example from Riverside.

School example: talking at home

'Enhancing oracy at home' is the subject of a bulletin sent home from the school. Talking points for families are provided, including questions to prompt debate about current news stories. Sentence starters and examples of oracy-focused praise help families tune into some of the criteria for effective speaking and listening and links are provided to relevant websites. The newsletter also features guidance on discussing different curriculum subjects, with open questions that can be used to encourage students to talk about their learning at home. The newsletter is part of Riverside's drive to involve families in its work on spoken language, a commitment that includes communication through texts, 'praise postcards' and Twitter. The school's oracy lead outlines another initiative:

'I introduced "table talk". The idea is to sit down together, have a meal and discuss your day. Everybody has a turn; nobody talks over one another and it's done in a pre-organized way with some questions to ask. I got loads of good feedback about what a great family time they had had. It's getting families on board and the students are realizing what they are doing in school can be brought home. Students need to be listened to at home as well as at school. Otherwise, we'll lose some of the power. They need to take it with them when they leave us and realize it's not just a school thing; it's a real-world thing.'

At primary level, similar efforts have been made to provide structure for students to talk and parents to ask about events at school. Queensway teachers, for example, send home sentence stems to prompt sharing, while at Rushton a parents' notice board outside the Year 1 classroom prompts 'Please ask your child about …' with links to current topics.

The examples here are all indicative of an asset-based view of families that assumes not only that they will want to support students' learning but also that homes are valuable contexts to practise talk in everyday, meaningful contexts. Many of the schools in this book serve diverse, multilingual communities, some of which have strong oral traditions in languages other than English. However, when transporting the talk routines of the classroom into the home, it is important to note that talk norms can vary considerably. Shirley Brice-Heath's influential work,[32] for example, reminds us that oral traditions of everyday language in many communities may differ markedly from those in schools, while still being both rich and functional. Similarly, broader conventions for communication can vary so that, in some communities, the linguistic devices associated with structured argumentation and prized in the classroom may be considered odd or even impolite.[33] Nevertheless, this connection of families to a school's spoken language work is an important part of a holistic view of its potential.

Questions for reflection

- How would you sum up your school's vision for the role of talk in learning?
- How does your school strike a balance between consistent routines and approaches to talk and teachers' professional judgement?
- How do you know if your students' proficiency in using talk is improving?

Further reading and resources

- Voice 21 provide examples of whole-school approaches to developing oracy, complete with video testimony from schools: https://voice21.org/teacher-talk-a-whole-school-approach-to-oracy/
- The University of Cambridge T-SEDA website provides details of the coding scheme and resources discussed in this chapter: http://bit.ly/T-SEDA.
- Voice 21 has a page with advice on assessing students' oracy: https://voice21.org/assessing-the-impact-of-oracy-on-your-students/

Moving forwards with classroom talk in practice

Chapter preview

This book began with a quotation which suggested that we could make a conscious choice to see student talk as a focus of attention – something to be taught explicitly and employed purposefully. This brief concluding chapter draws together the book's themes and revisits some of the key issues that have emerged from the glimpses into classroom practice. It covers:

- Revisiting the arguments for talk
- Moving towards a coherent model of classroom talk
- Looking ahead with new perspectives
- Last word

Revisiting the arguments for talk

Chapter 1 began in a classroom so, in keeping with the book's focus on practice, let's draw things together by visiting one more.

Classroom example

At Fairway, on a 'Talk Tuesday', students in Emma's Year 8 English class are consolidating their study of Romeo and Juliet. On the board is a stimulus for group discussion asking who was most responsible for the lovers' deaths. On the board are speech bubbles showing three fictional children's ideas. One speech bubble argues, for example, that Romeo and Juliet themselves were responsible, since they were not honest with their parents. Sentence stems provide possible ways of opening arguments and an additional challenge highlighted is to include in the discussions some key themes previously encountered in the text, such as feuding and melancholy.

Chairs are shifted into small groups of around four and heated debates begin. Forthright views about each of the three perspectives are shared, as some students jot down key prompts for themselves on mini whiteboards. After a few minutes, Emma interjects with a request for groups to reach consensus if at all possible, before resuming her circulation among the groups. As the group discussions come to a close and wider sharing begins, Emma first asks the students about the hallmarks of good listening, to which they reply with features such as eye contact and lack of fidgeting. In the subsequent whole-class plenary, Emma is able to facilitate without initially imposing her own views, due to her eavesdropping and awareness of each group's outcomes. She does this either by zooming in on productive debates ('Now, over here, you had some dispute, but what agreement did you eventually come to?') or by noticing connections ('This group, you also agreed with that view, didn't you? Take what they just said and add to it').

In the course of this book, extracts of classroom talk have been discussed under various chapter themes such as learning to talk, whole-class interaction, peer talk and so on. Of course, this thematic approach is somewhat arbitrary. It isolates aspects of practice for analysis from what are, in reality, complex classroom environments with many overlapping dynamics. For that reason, it is now important to integrate these themes, allowing us to interpret an episode like Emma's lesson in broader terms, such as the three key arguments put forward in Chapter 1, for example:

1 *The communicative competence argument*: Emma's lesson provides an opportunity for students to practise their spoken language, both in small groups and before the whole class. They are supported in this not only with sentence starters but also the explicit guidance on being a good listener. The request for group consensus places an extra demand on individuals' verbal reasoning and negotiation skills: simply agreeing to disagree will not do!

2 *The cognitive argument*: The initial stimulus immediately challenges students to consider multiple perspectives beyond their own first thoughts. In the subsequent exposure to peers' evidence-informed arguments, ideas but also ways of thinking through the issues are potentially appropriated. As the debate opens out to the class, elaboration and a build-up of collective understanding are sought.

3 *The student voice argument*: Fairway's Talk Tuesdays help legitimize student talk across the school. In this lesson, there is time and space to listen to and value diverse interpretations of a text. A safe space and intimate audience are provided in the small groups and Emma then skilfully invites particular contributions in the whole-class forum. The use of fictional characters' views as a stimulus helps to depersonalize the initial debate and encourage engagement.

Figure 4 A model of classroom talk

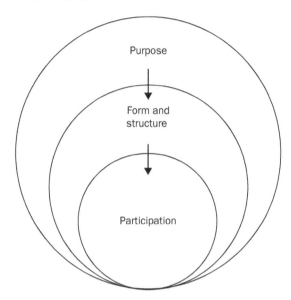

While the classrooms visited feature students from across England from the ages of 5 to 16, the book's approach has frequently been to juxtapose examples from contrasting settings and age groups to explore similarities in the principles underlying practice. With that in mind – and without downplaying age or subject differences – it is now possible to think about some fundamental features of talk practices in a more coherent way.

Moving towards a coherent model of classroom talk

Consider the three questions that were asked about the very first example in Chapter 1:

- *Why* are students talking?
- *How* are students talking?
- *Who* is talking and *to whom*?

Somewhat inspired by Alexander's approach to cross-cultural analysis of classrooms,[1] these three questions led in Chapter 1 directly to broad categories of *purpose, form* and *participation* and they might now be thought of as nested in a hierarchy of successive considerations, as shown in Figure 4.

The purpose of classroom talk

As a first consideration, it is important to be clear about the purpose for class-room talk. Chapter 2 noted overarching aims across schools which included raising attainment, developing life skills, closing an equity gap and valuing students' voices. These wide-ranging aims imply offering opportunities for talking for diverse purposes that range from the highly formal (think of Rushton's courtroom participants presenting arguments to the jury) to the messy and spontaneous (see Brookfield students' collective reasoning about an informal recording of ambiguous problems).

At the level of individual classrooms and lessons, however, teachers' professional judgement is paramount and in Chapter 8 this was illustrated by the underlying principle of *intentionality* used to guide practice at Eastland. Teachers' decision-making around the use of talk centres to a great extent on the idea of varied repertoires and the judicious choice of forms of interaction to serve a learning purpose. As discussed in Chapter 6, this includes decision-making about when learning needs suggest episodes that are more teacher-led or student-led. The extracts in this book, therefore, have seen talk used for a multitude of purposes. By way of illustration, consider for these pairs of superficially similar scenarios the contrasting purposes that were served by talk.

Responding to topical issues:

- Preparing formal presentations to argue persuasively for action on environmental issues (Chapter 3)
- Exploring personal views on drugs and alcohol through sharing experiences and values (Chapter 4).

Collaborating on a task in small groups:

- Problem-solving and troubleshooting to create a working computer output (Chapter 7)
- Inferring and speculating about fictional characters' actions by completing a SWOT analysis (Chapter 5).

Reasoning as a whole class:

- Building on and challenging peers' views to debate the issues around energy and poverty in an evidence-informed manner (Chapter 4)
- Sharing and evaluating strategies to solve a mathematics problem (Chapter 6).

If the learning purpose of talk is clear, then judgements on the form of talk that is appropriate can follow.

The form and structure of classroom talk

This book has illustrated a wide range of spoken language forms. Moving from the individual to the collective, they include, for example:

- Individual students speaking into a recording device to capture an explanation of their mathematical strategies (Chapter 7).
- Individual students presenting campaigning speeches to a whole-class audience (Chapter 3).
- Pairs of students discussing literary effects in a fiction text (Chapter 3).
- Small groups of students debating interpretations of historical events (Chapter 5).
- A whole-class open dialogue evaluating a school's sustainability activities (Chapter 6).
- A whole class considering the merits of autonomous vehicles using micro-blogging between groups (Chapter 7).
- Two classes discussing aspects of a film's plot and characters (Chapter 8).

In each case, it has also been shown how teachers overtly value, explicitly teach and collaboratively evaluate these specific forms of talk. Much of this practice depends on appropriate stimuli, guidance and resources to draw attention to spoken language as an object worthy of attention. These structures contribute to student participation in talk, which, as we have seen, includes active listening as well as vocal contributions.

Participation in classroom talk

The question of participation implies a concern for inclusion, a thread running through this book. The teachers encountered in this book had high expectations of participation and indeed often saw talk as a means to greater inclusion.
    In order to ensure participation, the book has shown teachers adopting three main approaches:

1 *Developing a collective ethos*: At whole-school level, oracy assemblies and common processes across the school model values and exemplify skills for teachers and students alike. At classroom level, there is an explicit commitment in many lessons to cumulative, constructive dialogue through the language of *building* on others' ideas and to the supporting of peers' understanding through explaining and rehearsing ideas in pairs.
2 *Putting into place structural scaffolds*: Across many of the lessons, similar structures support participation. They include the agreeing of ground rules, the teaching of discussion roles, the provision of sentence stems and specific vocabulary and the use of talk tokens.
3 *Maintaining an active and responsive role*: Teachers model and discuss effective spoken language use in an explicit way. They also act responsively to bridge between small groups and the whole class and to open up participation through skilled use of the 'third move' in whole-class discussion.

Revisiting a classroom example: integrating purpose, form and participation

The three components of purpose, form and participation can be illustrated through one of the lessons encountered. In Chapters 2 and 5 we met Isobel's Year 9 history students, in the midst of studying World War Two. Isobel had decided that, at that point in the unit, it was important for students to consider different interpretations of a contested historical issue through reasoned, evidence-informed debate (*purpose*). She determined that this would work best initially in small groups, based on provocative stimuli, specific talk tactics and the deployment of observers to note the verbal interaction within each group (*form*). Isobel's choice of small-group discussion was set within the context of a move within the subject area towards valuing talk, as exemplified through the introduction of oral assessments. The collective ethos was vividly emphasized through the time taken to understand and support a student who was reluctant to share ideas. Structure to support contributions was provided in the form of talk roles and sources of evidence and the small group sizes allowed for rehearsal of arguments in a relatively safe space. Isobel's role was also important, as she intervened frequently to move thinking on, ensuring that, through the group observers, attention was drawn to good models of speaking and listening (*participation*).

Looking ahead with new perspectives

As a final call to action, it is tempting to conclude the book with a list of 'easy wins' and some tips to implement tomorrow. However, while it is true that developing classroom talk can begin on a small scale in every classroom (and practical resources have been signposted in each chapter), the approach throughout has been to emphasize the importance of understanding the principles behind the practice, with a view to exercising professional judgement. It seems more fitting, therefore, to consider how the conditions for productive talk might be created by developing a particular *way of thinking* about this aspect of practice. To this end, it is possible to identify in the schools encountered a number of assumptions about learning and learners which have helped classroom talk to flourish.

Learning in a talk-rich classroom

First and foremost, learning to and through talk is not an add-on: it is deeply ingrained in the classrooms visited and this begins at the top of the school. Returning to some of the perceived challenges raised in Chapter 2 about curriculum coverage, evidence in books and a noisy classroom, there needs to be a form of accountability that acknowledges that silence, written work and teacher-led instruction are not always proxies for learning (though certainly each has its place). Within this learning environment, the valuing of talk is signalled explicitly through the physical classroom environment, in terms of displays and flexible seating arrangements, and through the teacher's feedback on process as well as product. The Year 1 sustainable development lesson in Chapter 6 is a vivid example of physical and visual cues to support discussion of the talk itself, as well as the substantive topic under consideration.

Learning, therefore, is understood to take many forms. Oral expression, peer collaboration and the co-construction of understanding are part of a rich diet that also includes teacher explanation, modelling and factual recall. Talk may be a common thread but the teacher's judgement in *blending* this mixture of forms according to the learning purpose is paramount. See, for example, the scaffolding with sentence stems in Year 8 English that allows for a more open exchange of ideas afterwards (Chapter 3) or the way that problem-solving discussion in computing builds on the necessary shared prior knowledge of programming (Chapter 7). Knowledge is not always a fixed entity but open to reasoned debate and interpretation, as seen in the Year 6 lesson on energy and poverty in Chapter 4.

The learner in a talk-rich classroom

Alongside these orientations to learning sit orientations to one's learners. A theme unifying the various motivations for promoting talk is a view of students as actively involved in their own learning. If understanding is at least partly co-constructed in these classrooms, then it follows that students need space to jointly consider and apply knowledge in novel ways, as seen in the Year 7 evaluation of autonomous vehicles in Chapter 7.

As well as these opportunities for consolidating learning, there needs to be a sense that students have something worthwhile to say that potentially goes beyond their time at school. Speaking out persuasively on real-life issues and in response to authentic questions, alongside articulating accepted curricular knowledge, is part of a student's learning for life. This has been illustrated, for example, by Underwood's focus on both local and global issues in Chapter 6 and by the Year 11 discussion of school-level change in Chapter 5. The value placed on these views is reinforced by the explicit teaching of listening as an essential skill.

This valuing of the learner's voice extends to an acknowledgment that talk is a multifaceted tool: as well as the formal register required in some settings and for some purposes, learners potentially bring many other communicative assets. Informal and sometimes idiosyncratic or local forms of speech have their place in learning and many of our classroom examples (such as the Year 9 mathematical discussions in Chapter 5) have allowed learners the messiness of more exploratory forms of talk.

Last word

In a book about classroom practice, it seems fitting to leave the last words to a classroom practitioner. A teacher at Woodham reflects on the transformative effect of a school-wide focus on talk:

> *Children are active participants in our classroom – everyone. There's not one lesson where children would be silent all lesson. Every child would speak multiple times in each lesson, whether to their partner or to the whole class. Every child is an active participant in the room. It blows my mind that there was a time when this didn't happen, when we had children who were silent for the whole of a lesson. I just find that so hard to believe.*

If the classrooms in this book have inspired you, then perhaps you can look forward to your own 'mind-blowing' journey into even more student participation and enhanced learning through spoken language. Let's keep the dialogue going!

Questions for reflection

- How might the ideas of purpose, form and function help you to begin planning for classroom talk?
- What assumptions about learning and learners now characterize your classroom and how do they, or might they, influence your daily practice?

Notes

Introduction: starting with the practice

1　Rosen and Rosen, 1973
2　e.g. Mercer and Littleton, 2007
3　e.g. Howe and Abedin, 2013
4　McIntyre, 2005
5　https://educationendowmentfoundation.org.uk/
6　https://ies.ed.gov/ncee/wwc/
7　Wrigley, 2018
8　Shulman and Wilson, 2004
9　Berliner, 2004
10　Hagger and McIntyre, 2006
11　Alexander, 2000, p. 269

Chapter 1: Making the case for classroom talk

1　Hymes, 1972; Bruner, 1978
2　CBI, 2019
3　Asmussen et al., 2019
4　Sutton Trust, 2012
5　Moll et al., 1992
6　Brice-Heath, 1983; Lareau, 2003; Delpit, 2006
7　Ofsted, 2021
8　DfE, 2013
9　Bourdieu, 1986
10　EEF, 2017; Howe et al., 2019; Sedova et al., 2019
11　Mercer and Littleton, 2007; Webb et al., 2017
12　Mercer, 2013
13　UNICEF, 1990
14　Lefstein and Snell, 2014
15　Mental Health Foundation, 2020
16　Alexander, 2019
17　Segal and Lefstein, 2016
18　Wilkinson, 1965
19　https://voice21.org/; https://www.esu.org/
20　Oracy APPG, 2021

21 Norman, 1992

22 Adapted from: https://voice21.org/wp-content/uploads/2020/06/Benchmarks-report-FINAL.pdf

23 e.g. Delpit, 2006

Chapter 2: Putting classroom talk into practice

1 Howe and Abedin, 2013; Alexander, 2020a

2 EEF, 2021

3 Greeno, 2015; Howe et al., 2019

4 Howe, 2014; Gillies, 2016

5 Mercer and Littleton, 2007

6 Alexander, 2020a

7 www.voice21.org

8 www.oracycambridge.org

9 https://ifl.pitt.edu/how-we-work/accountable-talks.cshtml

10 Dawes et al., 2004

11 Resnick et al., 2018

12 Lipman, 1998

13 Palinscar and Brown, 1984

14 Bullock, 1975

15 DfE, 2013; DfE, 2021

16 Carter, 1990; Norman, 1992

17 Jones, 2017; Alexander, 2020a

18 Oracy APPG, 2021

19 Law et al., 2017

20 Millard and Menzies, 2016

21 Snell and Lefstein, 2018

22 Alexander, 2020a

23 Alexander, 2000

24 Mercer et al, 2017

25 Voice 21, 2020a

26 Cameron, 2003; Alexander, 2020a

27 Voice 21, 2019

Chapter 3: Learning to talk and listen

1 CBI, 2019

2 Van der Wilt et al., 2016

3 Snowling et al., 2011; Law et al., 2017; Asmussen et al., 2019

4 Centre for Social Justice, 2014

5 Wilkinson, 1965
6 Mercer, 2018
7 Alexander, 2020a
8 Hymes, 1972
9 Dockerell et al., 2012; Millard and Menzies, 2016
10 Gilkerson et al., 2018
11 Brice-Heath, 1983; Lareau, 2003
12 Fisher and Larkin, 2008; Coultas, 2015
13 Mercer et al., 2017
14 Nuthall, 2004
15 Gaunt and Stott, 2019
16 Romeo et al., 2018; Gilkerson et al., 2018
17 Gripton and Knight, 2020
18 Wood et al., 1976, p. 90
19 Wertsch, 2008
20 Wood et al., 1976
21 van de Pol et al., 2010
22 EEF, 2018; Perry et al., 2018
23 Reznitskaya and Gregory, 2013
24 https://thinkingtogether.educ.cam.ac.uk/resources/
25 Jackson, 1968
26 Flavell, 1979
27 EEF, 2018
28 Zepeda et al., 2019
29 Mercer et al., 2017; EEF, 2018
30 EEF, 2021
31 Perry et al., 2018; Visible Learning, 2018
32 https://thinkingtogether.educ.cam.ac.uk/resources/
33 Newman, 2017
34 Visible Learning, 2018; Alexander, 2020a
35 Oracy APPG, 2021
36 Bernstein, 1971
37 Delpit, 2006, p. 40
38 Brice-Heath, 1983; Lareau, 2003
39 Lareau, 2003
40 Cushing, 2019
41 Barnes, 1976
42 Gaunt and Stott, 2019
43 Mercer, 2000, p. 162
44 Lambirth, 2009

45 Barak and Lefstein, 2022
46 Yang, 2016
47 Mercer and Littleton, 2007

Chapter 4: Talking with the teacher as a whole class
 1 Flanders, 1961; Galton et al., 1999; Burns and Myhill, 2004
 2 Teo, 2016; Chan, 2020
 3 Millard and Menzies, 2016; Teo, 2016
 4 Cazden, 2001; Howe and Abedin, 2013; Muhonen et al., 2022
 5 Moreira et al., 2019
 6 Alexander, 2020a
 7 Nystrand et al., 2003
 8 Mercer and Littleton, 2007
 9 Mehan and Cazden, 2015, p. 19
10 Howe et al., 2019
11 Michaels and O'Connor, 2015
12 Edwards, 1992
13 Smith et al., 2004; Vaish, 2008
14 Fisher, 2009; Biggs and Tang, 2011
15 Wood, 1992
16 Nystrand and Gamoran, 1997, p. 72
17 Nystrand and Gamoran, 1997; Nystrand et al., 2003; Applebee et al., 2003
18 Nystrand and Gamoran, 1997, p. 72
19 Snell and Lefstein, 2018
20 Rowe, 1978
21 Lefstein and Snell, 2014
22 Segal and Lefstein, 2016
23 Applebee et al., 2003; Mercer and Littleton, 2007; Alexander, 2018
24 Sedova et al., 2019
25 O'Connor et al., 2017
26 Sedova and Navratilova, 2020
27 Alexander, 2000
28 Alexander, 2000, p. 454
29 Sinclair and Coulthard, 1975
30 e.g. Mercer and Littleton, 2007
31 Howe et al., 2019
32 Hennessy et al., 2021
33 Lefstein, 2010
34 Mercer, 2000
35 Michaels et al., 2016

36   Mercer and Littleton, 2007; Howe et al., 2019
37   Greeno, 2015
38   Carter and McCarthy, 1995
39   e.g. Bercow, 2008; EEF, 2021
40   Corbett and Strong, 2017
41   Myhill and Newman, 2016

Chapter 5: Talking with peers

1   Alexander, 2020a
2   Bennett, 2019
3   Rojas-Drummond and Mercer, 2003; Mercer and Littleton, 2007; Rojas-Drummond et al., 2014
4   Reznitskaya et al., 2009; Murphy et al., 2009; Sun et al., 2015
5   Palinscar and Brown, 1984; Gillies, 2016
6   Barnes, 1976
7   Mercer, 2000, p. 98
8   Littleton and Mercer, 2013
9   Mercer and Dawes, 2008; Gillies, 2016
10   Dawes et al., 2004; Gillies, 2016; Mercer et al., 2017
11   Webb et al., 2014; Gillies, 2016
12   Kirschner et al., 2018; Willingham, 2007
13   Vygotsky, 1978
14   Mercer, 2000; Mercer and Littleton, 2007
15   Littleton and Mercer, 2013
16   Barnes, 1976
17   Barnes, 1976 p. 28
18   Mercer, 2000
19   Mercer and Littleton, 2007; Reznitskaya et al., 2009; Sun et al., 2015
20   Mercer, 2013
21   Kirschner et al., 2018
22   Nystrand and Gamoran, 1997
23   Willingham, 2007
24   e.g. Mercer and Littleton, 2007; Gillies, 2016; Mercer et al., 2017
25   e.g. Gaunt and Stott, 2019
26   Wegerif, 2010
27   Dawes et al., 2004; Mercer and Littleton, 2007
28   Rojas-Drummond and Mercer, 2003; Mercer and Littleton, 2007; Rojas-Drummond et al., 2014
29   Grice, 1975

30 Mercer, 2000
31 Gillies, 2016, p. 26
32 Dawes et al., 2004
33 Reznitskaya et al., 2009
34 Palinscar and Brown, 1984
35 e.g. Tan, 2019
36 Kirschner et al., 2006; Sweller, 2016
37 Gillies, 2016
38 Reznitskaya et al., 2009
39 Adey and Shayer, 2015
40 Adey, 2008, p. 49
41 Howe, 2021

Chapter 6: Moving towards a dialogic classroom

1 Alexander, 2020a
2 Alexander, 2020a
3 Alexander, 2020a, p. 2
4 Lefstein and Snell, 2011; Boyd and Markarian, 2011
5 Alexander, 2020a; https://robinalexander.org.uk/dialogic-teaching/ (accessed 23 March 2021)
6 Mortimer and Scott, 2003; Mercer and Littleton, 2007
7 Nystrand et al., 2003; Mercer et al., 2009; Reznitskaya and Gregory, 2013
8 Kim and Wilkinson, 2019
9 Cui and Teo, 2021
10 Applebee et al., 2003; Howe et al., 2019
11 O'Connor et al., 2015; EEF, 2017
12 Alexander, 2020a
13 Kim and Wilkinson, 2019
14 Alexander, 2020a
15 O'Connor and Michaels, 2007
16 Wells and Arauz, 2006
17 Boyd and Markarian, 2015
18 Alexander, 2020a
19 Alexander, 2020a
20 Resnick et al., 2018
21 Michaels et al., 2016, p. 12
22 e.g. Reznitskaya and Gregory, 2013
23 Nystrand et al., 2003
24 Snell and Lefstein, 2018

25 Wells and Arauz, 2006
26 Mortimer and Scott, 2003, p. 35
27 Mercer, 2015
28 Segal and Lefstein, 2016, p. 16
29 Lefstein and Snell, 2011
30 Freire, 1970
31 Wegerif, 2020
32 e.g. Willingham, 2007
33 Reznitskaya et al., 2012
34 Trickey and Topping, 2004; Topping and Trickey, 2014
35 Voice 21, 2019

Chapter 7: Talking with digital technology

1 Hennessy et al., 2018
 2 Wegerif, 2020
 3 Major et al., 2018
 4 Hennessy et al., 2018; Major et al., 2018
 5 Wegerif and Dawes, 2004
 6 Wegerif, 2007
 7 Hennessy et al., 2018
 8 Littleton and Mercer, 2013
 9 Cook et al., 2019; Asterhan, 2015
10 Major et al., 2018
11 Darling-Hammond and Hyler, 2020
12 Oracy APPG, 2021
13 Voice 21, 2020b
14 https://www.youtube.com/watch?v=Bl1FOKpFY2Q
15 Dawes, 2008
16 Naylor and Keogh, 2013
17 Hennessy, 2011
18 Cook et al., 2019; Frøytlog and Rasmussen, 2020; Warwick et al., 2020
19 Warwick et al., 2020
20 Frøytlog and Rasmussen, 2020
21 Wegerif, 2007
22 Wegerif and Dawes, 2004; Mercer and Littleton, 2007
23 Littleton and Mercer, 2013
24 Barnes, 1976, p.108
25 e.g. Alexander, 2018; Lefstein and Snell, 2014
26 Major et al., 2018

Chapter 8: Sustaining classroom talk across the school

1 McIntyre, 2005; Nuthall, 2004
2 Hargreaves, 2016; Solomon and Lewin, 2016
3 Fullan, 2016
4 Hargreaves, 2016
5 Darling-Hammond, 2017
6 EEF, 2019
7 Lefstein, 2010
8 Alexander, 2020a
9 Voice 21 website impact page: https://voice21.org/impact/
10 Osborne et al., 2013
11 Oracy APPG, 2021
12 Fullan and Hargreaves, 2012
13 Fullan and Hargreaves, 2012, p. 3
14 Osborne et al., 2013, p. 338
15 Hargreaves, 2016
16 Bullock, 1975
17 Bercow, 2008
18 Oracy APPG, 2021
19 Osborne et al., 2013; Hennessy et al., 2018; Alexander, 2018
20 Hennessy et al., 2018, p. 149
21 Michaels et al., 2016
22 Michaels et al., 2016, p. 15
23 Black and Wiliam, 2018
24 Education.gouv.fr, 2022
25 Alexander, 2020b
26 Mercer et al., 2017
27 Mercer et al., 2017
28 Hennessy et al., 2016; Hennessy et al., 2020
29 T-SEDA Collective, 2021
30 Ahmed, 2017
31 Moll et al., 1992
32 Brice-Heath, 1983
33 Michaels et al., 2016

Chapter 9: Moving forwards with classroom talk

1 Alexander, 2000

References

Adey, P. (ed.) (2008) *Let's Think Handbook: A Guide to Cognitive Acceleration in the Primary School*. London: GL Assessment.

Adey, P. and Shayer, M. (2015) The effects of cognitive acceleration, in L. Resnick, C. Asterhan and S. Clarke (eds) *Socializing Intelligence Through Academic Talk and Dialogue*, 127–40. Washington, DC: American Educational Research Association.

Ahmed, A. (2017) *Should we assess oracy and can comparative judgement help?* Available at: https://oracycambridge.org/should-we-assess-oracy-and-can-comparative-judgement-help/ (accessed 18 April 2022).

Alexander, R. (2000) *Culture and Pedagogy: International Comparisons in Primary Education*. Oxford: Blackwell.

Alexander, R. (2018) Developing dialogic teaching: genesis, process, trial, *Research Papers in Education*, 33(5): 561–98.

Alexander, R. (2019) Whose discourse? Dialogic pedagogy for a post-truth world, *Dialogic Pedagogy* 7. Available at: https://dpj.pitt.edu/ojs/index.php/dpj1/article/view/268 (accessed 18 April 2022).

Alexander, R. (2020a) *A Dialogic Teaching Companion*. Abingdon: Routledge.

Alexander, R. (2020b) *Oracy All-Party Parliamentary Group oral evidence*, 14 July 2020. Available at: www.youtube.com/watch?v=mkjCk3s9abwandt=537s (accessed 18 April 2022).

Applebee, A., Langer, J., Nystrand, M. et al. (2003) Discussion-based approaches to developing understanding: classroom instruction and student performance in middle and high school English, *American Educational Research Journal*, 40(3): 685–730.

Asmussen, K., Law, J., Charlton, J. et al. (2019) *Key competencies in early cognitive development: things, people, numbers and words*. Available at: www.eif.org.uk/report/key-competencies-in-early-cognitive-development-things-people-numbers-and-words (accessed 18 April 2022).

Asterhan, C. (2015) Introducing online dialogues in co-located classrooms: if, why and how, in L. Resnick, C. Asterhan and S. Clarke (eds) *Socializing Intelligence Through Academic Talk and Dialogue*, 205–18. Washington, DC: American Educational Research Association.

Barak, M. and Lefstein, A. (2022) Above the law? The democratic implications of setting ground rules for dialogue, *Language and Education*, 36(3): 195–210.

Barnes, D. (1976) *From Communication to Curriculum*. London: Penguin.

Bennett, T. (2019) Foreword, in A. Boxer (ed.) *The ResearchED Guide to Explicit and Direct Instruction*. Woodbridge, Suffolk: John Catt.

Bercow, J. (2008) *The Bercow Report: A Review of Services for Children and Young People (0–19) with Speech, Language and Communication Needs*. London: Department for Children Schools and Families (DCSF). Available at: https://dera.ioe.ac.uk/8405/7/7771-dcsf-bercow_Redacted.pdf (accessed 18 April 2022).

Berliner, D. (2004) Describing the behavior and documenting the accomplishments of expert teachers, *Bulletin of Science, Technology and Society*, 24(3): 200–12.

Bernstein, B. (1971) *Class, Codes and Control*. London: Routledge.

Biggs, J. and Tang. C. (2011) *Teaching for Quality Learning at University*, 4th edn. Maidenhead: Open University Press.

Black, P. and Wiliam, D. (2018) Classroom assessment and pedagogy, *Assessment in Education: Principles, Policy and Practice*, 25(6): 551–75.

Bourdieu, P. (1986) The forms of capital, in J. Richardson (ed.), *Handbook of Theory and Research for the Sociology of Education*, 241–58. Westport, CT: Greenwood.

Boyd, M. and Markarian, W. (2011) Dialogic teaching: talk in service of a dialogic stance, *Language and Education*, 25(6): 515–34.

Boyd, M. and Markarian, W. (2015) Teaching and dialogic stance: moving beyond inter-actional form, *Research in the Teaching of English*, 49(3): 272–96.

Brice-Heath, S. (1983) *Ways With Words: Language, Life and Work in Communities and Classrooms*. Cambridge: Cambridge University Press.

Bruner, J. (1978) The role of dialogue in language acquisition, in A. Sinclair, R. Jevella and W. Levelt (eds) *The Child's Conception of Language*, 241–56. Berlin: Springer-Verlag.

Bullock, A. (1975) *The Bullock Report: A Language for Life: Report of the Committee of Enquiry Appointed by the Secretary of State for Education and Science under the Chairmanship of Sir Alan Bullock FBA*. London: HMSO.

Burns, C. and Myhill, D. (2004) Interactive or inactive? A consideration of the nature of interaction in whole class teaching, *Cambridge Journal of Education*, 34(1): 35–49.

Cameron, D. (2003) Schooling spoken language: beyond 'communication', in Qualifications and Curriculum Authority (ed.) *New Perspectives on English in the Classroom*, 64–72. London: QCA.

Carter, R. (1990) *Knowledge About Language and the Curriculum: The LINC Reader*. London: Hodder and Stoughton.

Carter, R. and McCarthy, M. (1995) Grammar and the spoken language, *Applied Linguistics*, 16(2): 141–58.

Cazden, C. (2001) *Classroom Discourse: The Language of Teaching and Learning*, 2nd edn. Portsmouth, NH: Heinemann.

CBI (2019) *Education and Learning for the Modern World: CBI/Pearson Education and Skills Survey Report 2019*. Available at: www.cbi.org.uk/media/3841/12546_tess_2019. pdf (accessed 18 April 2022).

Centre for Social Justice (2014) *Closing the Divide: Tackling Educational Inequality in England*. Centre for Social Justice. Available at: www.centreforsocialjustice.org.uk/library/closing-divide-tackling-educational-inequality-england (accessed 18 April 2022).

Chan, M. (2020) A multilevel SEM study of classroom talk on cooperative learning and aca-demic achievement: does cooperative scaffolding matter?, *International Journal of Educational Research*, https://doi.org/10.1016/j.ijer.2020.101564 (accessed 28 July 2022).

Cook, V., Warwick, P., Vrikki, M. et al. (2019) Developing material-dialogic space in geog-raphy learning and teaching: combining a dialogic pedagogy with the use of a microb-logging tool, *Thinking Skills and Creativity*, 31: 217–31.

Corbett, P. and Strong, J. (2017) *Talk for Writing Across the Curriculum*, 2nd edn. Maid-enhead: Open University Press.

Coultas, V. (2015) Revisiting debates on oracy: classroom talk – moving towards a dem-ocratic pedagogy?, *Changing English*, 22(1): 72–86.

Cui, R. and Teo, P. (2021) Dialogic education for classroom teaching: a critical review, *Language and Education*, 35(3): 187–203.

Cushing, I. (2019) The policy and policing of language in schools, *Language and Society*, 49: 425–50.

Darling-Hammond, L. (2017) Teacher education around the world: what can we learn from international practice?, *European Journal of Teacher Education*, 40(3): 291–309.

Darling-Hammond, L. and Hyler, M. (2020) Preparing educators for the time of COVID … and beyond, *European Journal of Teacher Education*, 43(4): 457–65.

Dawes, L. (2008) *The Essential Speaking and Listening: Talk for Learning at Key Stage 2*. London: David Fulton.

Dawes, L., Mercer, N. and Wegerif, R. (2004) *Thinking Together: A Programme of Activities for Developing Speaking, Listening and Thinking Skills for Children Aged 8–11*. Birmingham: Imaginative Minds.

Delpit, L. (2006) *Other People's Children*. New York: The New Press.

Department for Education (2013) *National Curriculum in England: English Programmes of Study*. Available at: www.gov.uk/government/publications/national-curriculum-in-england-english-programmes-of-study (accessed 18 April 2022).

Department for Education (2021) *Statutory Framework for the Early Years Foundation Stage: Setting the Standards for Learning, Development and Care for Children from Birth to Five*. Available at: https://assets.publishing.service.gov.uk/government/uploads/system/uploads/attachment_data/file/974907/EYFS_framework_-_March_2021.pdf (accessed 18 April 2022).

Dockrell, J., Bakopoulou, I., Law, J. et al. (2012) *Developing a Communication Supporting Classrooms Observation Tool*. Available at: https://dera.ioe.ac.uk/16319/1/DFE-RR247-BCRP8.pdf (accessed 18 April 2022).

Education Endowment Foundation (2017) *Dialogic Teaching: Evaluation Report and Executive Summary*. London: Education Endowment Foundation.

Education Endowment Foundation (2018) *Metacognition and Self-regulation: Teaching and Learning Toolkit*. Available at: https://educationendowmentfoundation.org.uk/pdf/generate/?u=https://educationendowmentfoundation.org.uk/pdf/toolkit/?id=138andt=Teaching%20and%20Learning%20Toolkitande=138ands= (accessed 18 April 2022).

Education Endowment Foundation (2019) *Putting Evidence to Work: A School's Guide to Implementation*. Available at: https://educationendowmentfoundation.org.uk/education-evidence/guidance-reports/implementation (accessed 18 April 2022).

Education Endowment Foundation (2021) *Oral Language Interventions: Teaching and Learning Toolkit*. Available at: https://educationendowmentfoundation.org.uk/education-evidence/teaching-learning-toolkit/oral-language-interventions (accessed 18 April 2022).

Education.gouv.fr (2022) *Baccalaureate: How is the Grand Oral going?* Available at: https://www.education.gouv.fr/reussir-au-lycee/baccalaureat-comment-se-passe-le-grand-oral-100028 (accessed 18 April 2022).

Edwards, T. (1992) Teacher talk and pupil competence, in K. Norman (ed.) *Thinking Voices: The Work of the National Oracy Project*, 235–42. London: Hodder and Stoughton.

Fisher, R. (2009) *Creative Dialogue: Talk for Thinking in the Classroom*. Abingdon: Routledge.

Fisher, R. and Larkin, S. (2008) Pedagogy or ideological struggle? An examination of pupils' and teachers' expectations for talk in the classroom, *Language and Education*, 22(1): 1–16.

Flanders, N. (1961) Analysing teacher behaviour, *Educational Leadership*, December 1961: 173–200.

Flavell, J. (1979) Metacognition and cognitive monitoring: a new area of cognitive-developmental inquiry, *American Psychologist*, 34(10): 906–11.

Freire, P. (1970) *Pedagogy of the Oppressed*. London: Penguin.

Frøytlog, J. and Rasmussen, I. (2020) The distribution and productivity of whole-class dialogues: exploring the potential of microblogging, *International Journal of Educational Research*, 99: 101501.

Fullan, M. (2016) *The New Meaning of Educational Change*, 5th edn. Abingdon: Routledge.

Fullan, M. and Hargreaves, A. (2012) *Professional Capital: Transforming Teaching in Every School*. Abingdon: Routledge.

Galton, M., Hargreaves, L., Comber, C. et al. (1999) Changes in patterns of teacher interaction in primary classrooms 1976–96, *British Educational Research Journal*, 25(1): 23–37.

Gaunt, A. and Stott, A. (2019) *Transform Teaching and Learning Through Talk: The Oracy Imperative*. London: Rowman and Littlefield.

Gilkerson, J., Richards, J., Warren, S. et al. (2018) Language experience in the second year of life and language outcomes in late childhood, *Pediatrics*, 142(4): 1–11.

Gillies, R. (2016) *Enhancing Classroom-based Talk: Blending Practice, Research and Theory*. Abingdon: Routledge.

Greeno, J. (2015) Classroom talk sequences and learning, in L. Resnick, C. Asterhan and S. Clarke (eds) *Socializing Intelligence Through Academic Talk and Dialogue*, 255–62. Washington, DC: American Educational Research Association.

Grice, H. P. (1975) Logic and conversation, in P. Cole and J. Morgan (eds) *Speech Acts* [*Syntax and Semantics* 3], 41–58. New York: Academic Press.

Gripton, C. and Knight, R. (2020) Walking the talk: moving forwards with sustained shared thinking and dialogic teaching, *Forum*, 62(1): 31–40.

Hagger, H. and McIntyre, D. (2006) *Learning Teaching from Teachers: Realizing the Potential of School-based Teacher Education*. Maidenhead: Open University Press.

Hargreaves, D. (2016) Autonomy and transparency: two good ideas gone bad, in J. Evers and R. Kneyber (eds) *Flip the System: Changing Education from the Ground Up*, 120–33. Abingdon: Routledge.

Hennessy, S. (2011) The role of digital artefacts on the interactive whiteboard in supporting classroom dialogue, *Journal of Computer Assisted Learning*, 27: 463–89.

Hennessy, S., Calcagni, E., Leung, A. and Mercer, N. (2021) An analysis of the forms of teacher–student dialogue that are most productive for learning, *Language and Education*. Available at: https://doi.org/10.1080/09500782.2021.1956943.

Hennessy, S., Rojas-Drummond, S., Higham, R. et al. (2016) Developing a coding scheme for analysing classroom dialogue across educational contexts, *Learning, Culture and Social Interaction*, 9: 16–44.

Hennessy, S., Dragovic, T. and Warwick, P. (2018) A research informed, school-based professional development workshop programme to promote dialogic teaching with interactive technologies, *Professional Development in Education*, 44(2): 145–68.

Hennessy, S., Howe, C., Mercer, N. and Vrikki, M. (2020) Coding classroom dialogue: methodological considerations for researchers, *Learning, Culture and Social Interaction*, 25: 100404.

Howe, C. (2021) Strategies for supporting the transition from small group activity to student learning: a possible role for beyond group sharing, *Learning, Culture and Social Interaction*, 28: 100471.

Howe, C. (2014) Optimizing small group discourse in classrooms: effective practices and theoretical constraints, *International Journal of Education Research*, 63: 107–15.

Howe, C. and Abedin, M. (2013) Classroom dialogue: a systematic review across four decades of research, *Cambridge Journal of Education*, 43(3): 325–56.

Howe, C., Hennessy, S., Mercer, N. et al. (2019) Teacher–student dialogue during classroom teaching: does it really impact on student outcomes?, *Journal of the Learning Sciences*, 28(4–5): 462–512.

Hymes, D. (1972) On communicative competence, in J. Pride and J. Holmes (eds) *Sociolinguistics*, 269–93. London: Penguin.

Jackson, P. (1968) *Life in Classrooms*. New York: Holt, Reinhart and Winston.

Jones, D. (2017) Talking about talk: reviewing oracy in English primary education, *Early Child Development and Care*, 187(3–4): 498–508.

Kim, M. and Wilkinson, I. (2019) What is dialogic teaching? Constructing, deconstructing, and reconstructing a pedagogy of classroom talk, *Learning, Culture and Social Interaction*, 21: 70–86.

Kirschner, P., Sweller, J. and Clark, R. (2006) Why minimal guidance during instruction does not work: an analysis of the failure of constructivist, discovery, problem-based, experiential and inquiry-based learning, *Educational Psychologist*, 41(2): 75–86.

Kirschner, P., Sweller, J., Kirschner, F. and Zambrano, J. (2018) From cognitive load theory to collaborative cognitive load theory, *International Journal of Computer Supported Collaborative Learning*, 13: 213–33.

Lambirth, A. (2009) Ground rules for talk: the acceptable face of prescription, *The Curriculum Journal*, 20(4): 423–35.

Lareau, A. (2003) *Unequal Childhoods*. Berkeley, CA: University of California Press.

Law, J., Charlton, J. and Asmussen, K. (2017) *Language as a Child Wellbeing Indicator*, Early Intervention Foundation. Available at: https://www.eif.org.uk/files/pdf/language-child-wellbeing-indicator.pdf (accessed 18 April 2022).

Lefstein, A. (2010) More helpful as problem than solution: some implications of situating dialogue in classrooms, in K. Littleton and C. Howe (eds) *Educational Dialogues: Understanding and Promoting Productive Interaction*. Routledge: London.

Lefstein, A. and Snell, J. (2011) Classroom dialogue: the promise and complexity of dialogic practice, in S. Ellis and E. McCartney (eds) *Applied Linguistics and Primary School Teaching: Developing a Language Curriculum*, 165–85. Cambridge: Cambridge University Press.

Lefstein, A. and Snell, J. (2014) *Better Than Best Practice: Developing Teaching and Learning Through Dialogue*. Abingdon: Routledge.

Lipman, M. (1998) Teaching students to think reasonably: some findings of the philosophy for children program, *The Clearing House: A Journal of Educational Strategies, Issues and Ideas*, 71(5): 277–280.

Littleton, K. and Mercer, N. (2013) *Interthinking: Putting Talk to Work*. Abingdon: Routledge.

Major, L., Warwick, P., Rasmussen, I. et al. (2018) Classroom dialogue and digital technologies: a scoping review, *Educational Information Technology*, 23: 1995–2028.

McIntyre, D. (2005) Bridging the gap between research and practice, *Cambridge Journal of Education*, 35(3): 357–82.

Mehan, H. and Cazden, C. (2015) The study of classroom discourse: early history and current developments, in L. Resnick, C. Asterhan and S. Clarke (eds) *Socializing Intelligence Through Academic Talk and Dialogue*, 13–34. Washington, DC: American Educational Research Association.

Mental Health Foundation (2020) *Returning to School After the Coronavirus Lockdown*. Available at: www.mentalhealth.org.uk/coronavirus/returning-school-after-lockdown (accessed 18 April 2022).

Mercer, N. (2000) *Words and Minds: How We Use Language to Think Together*. London: Routledge.

Mercer, N. (2013) The social brain, language and goal-directed collective thinking: a social conception of cognition and its implications for understanding how we think, teach and learn, *Educational Psychologist*, 48(3): 148–68.

Mercer, N. (2015) Why oracy must be in the curriculum (and group work in the classroom), *Forum*, 57(1): 67–74.

Mercer, N. (2018) *Oracy education and dialogic teaching: what's the difference?* Available at: https://oracycambridge.org/oracy-education-and-dialogic-teaching-whats-the-difference/ (accessed 18 April 2022).

Mercer, N. and Dawes, L. (2008) The value of exploratory talk, in N. Mercer and S. Hodkinson (eds) *Exploring Talk in School*, 55–72. London: Sage.

Mercer, N., Dawes, L. and Kleine Staarman, J. (2009) Dialogic teaching in the primary science classroom, *Language and Education*, 23(4): 353–69.

Mercer, N. and Littleton, K. (2007) *Dialogue and the Development of Children's Thinking: A Sociocultural Approach*. Abingdon: Routledge.

Mercer, N., Warwick, P. and Ahmed, A. (2017) An oracy assessment toolkit: linking research and development in the assessment of students' spoken language skills at age 11–12, *Learning and Instruction*, 48: 51–60.

Michaels, S. and O'Connor, C. (2015) Conceptualizing talk moves as tools: professional development approaches for academically productive discussions, in L. Resnick, C. Asterhan and S. Clarke (eds) *Socializing Intelligence Through Academic Talk and Dialogue*, 347–61. Washington, DC: American Educational Research Association.

Michaels, S., O'Connor, C., Hall, M. and Resnick, L. (2016) *Accountable Talk Sourcebook: For Classroom Conversation that Works*. Available at: https://nsiexchange.org/wp-content/uploads/2019/02/AT-SOURCEBOOK2016-1-23-19.pdf (accessed 25 July 2022).

Millard, W. and Menzies, L. (2016) *Oracy: The State of Speaking in our Schools*, London: Voice 21. Available at: https://cfey.org/wp-content/uploads/2016/11/Oracy-Report-Final.pdf (accessed 28 July 2022).

Moll, L., Amanti, C., Neff, D. and Gonzalez, N. (1992) Funds of knowledge for teaching: using a qualitative approach to connect homes and classrooms, *Theory into Practice*, 31(2): 132–41.

Moreira, B., Pinto, T., Starling, D. and Jaeger, A. (2019) Retrieval practice in classroom settings: a review of applied research, *Frontiers in Education*, 4(5). Available at: https://doi.org/10.3389/feduc.2019.00005.

Mortimer, E. and Scott, P. (2003) *Meaning Making in Secondary Science Classrooms*. Maidenhead: Open University Press.

Muhonen, H., Verma, P., von Suchodoletz, A. and Rasku-Puttonen, H. (2022) Exploring types of educational classroom talk in early childhood education centres, *Research Papers in Education*, 37(1): 30–51.

Murphy, P., Wilkinson, I., Soter, A. and Hennessey, M. (2009) Examining the effects of classroom discussion on students' comprehension of text: a meta-analysis, *Journal of Educational Psychology*, 101(3): 740–64.

Myhill, D. and Newman, R. (2016) Metatalk: enabling metalinguistic discussion about writing, *International Journal of Educational Research*, 80: 177–87.

Naylor, S. and Keogh, B. (2013) Concept cartoons: what have we learnt?, *Journal of Turkish Science Education*, 10(1): 3–11.

Newman, R. (2017) Engaging talk: one teacher's scaffolding of collaborative talk, *Language and Education*, 31(2): 130–51.

Norman, K. (ed.) (1992) *Thinking Voices: The Work of the National Oracy Project*. London: Hodder and Stoughton.

Nuthall, G. (2004) Relating classroom teaching to student learning: a critical analysis of why research has failed to bridge the theory–practice gap, *Harvard Educational Review*, 74(3): 273–306.

Nystrand, M. and Gamoran, A. (1997) The big picture: language and learning in hundreds of English lessons, in M. Nystrand, A. Gamoran, R. Kachur and C. Prendergast, *Opening Dialogue: Understanding the Dynamics of Language and Learning in the English Classroom*. New York: Teachers College Press.

Nystrand, M., Wu, L., Gamoran, A., Zeisler, S. and Long, D. (2003) Questions in time: investigating the structure and dynamics of unfolding classroom discourse, *Discourse Processes*, 35(2): 135–98.

O'Connor, C. and Michaels, S. (2007) When is dialogue dialogic?, *Human Development*, 50: 275–85.

O'Connor, C., Michaels, S. and Chapin, S. (2015) 'Scaling down' to explore the role of talk in learning: from district intervention to controlled classroom study, in L. Resnick, C. Asterhan and S. Clarke (eds) *Socializing Intelligence Through Academic Talk and Dialogue*, 111–26. Washington, DC: American Educational Research Association.

O'Connor, C., Michaels, S., Chapin, S. and Harbaugh, A. (2017) The silent and the vocal: participation and learning in whole-class discussion, *Learning and Instruction*, 48: 5–13.

Ofsted (2021) *Education Inspection Framework*. Available at: www.gov.uk/government/publications/education-inspection-framework (accessed 18 April 2022).

Oracy All-Party Parliamentary Group (2021) *Speak for Change: Final Report and Recommendations from the Oracy All-Party Parliamentary Group Inquiry*. Available at: https://oracy.inparliament.uk/sites/oracy.inparliament.uk/files/2021-04/Oracy_APPG_FinalReport_28_04%20%281%29.pdf (accessed 18 April 2022).

Osborne, J., Simon, S., Christodolou, A., Howell-Richardson, C. and Richardson, K. (2013) Learning to Argue: A study of four schools and their attempt to develop the use of argumentation as a common instructional practice and its impact on students, *Journal of Research in Science Teaching*, 50(3): 315–47.

Palinscar, A. and Brown, A. (1984) Reciprocal teaching of comprehension-fostering and comprehension-monitoring activities, *Cognition and Instruction*, 1(2): 117–75.

Perry, J., Lundie, D. and Golder, G. (2018) Metacognition in schools: what does the literature suggest about the effectiveness of teaching metacognition in schools?, *Educational Review*, 71(4): 483–500.

Resnick, L., Asterhan, C. and Clarke, S. (2018) *Educational Practices Series 29: Accountable talk: instructional dialogue that builds the mind*. Available at: http://www.ibe.unesco.org/sites/default/files/resources/educational_practices_29-v7_002.pdf (accessed 18 April 2022).

Reznitskaya, A., Glina, M., Carolan, B. et al. (2012) Examining transfer effects from dialogic discussions to new tasks and contexts, *Contemporary Educational Psychology*, 37(4): 288–306.

Reznitskaya, A. and Gregory, M. (2013) Student thought and classroom language: examining the mechanisms of change in dialogic teaching, *Educational Psychologist*, 48(2): 114–33.

Reznityskaya, A., Kuo, L., Clark, A. et al. (2009) Collaborative reasoning: a dialogic approach to group discussions, *Cambridge Journal of Education*, 39(1): 29–48.

Rojas-Drummond, S. and Mercer, N. (2003) Scaffolding the development of effective collaboration and learning, *International Journal of Educational Research*, 39(1–2): 99–111.

Rojas-Drummond, S., Mazon, N., Littleton, K. and Velez, M. (2014) Developing reading comprehension through collaborative learning, *Journal of Research in Reading*, 37(2): 138–158.

Romeo, R., Leonard, J., Robinson, S. et al. (2018) Beyond the 30-million word gap: children's conversational exposure is associated with language-related brain function, *Psychological Science*, 29(5): 700–10.

Rosen, C. and Rosen, H. (1973) *The Language of Primary School Children*. London: Penguin.

Rowe, M. (1978) *Teaching Science as Continuous Inquiry*. New York: McGraw-Hill.

Sahlberg, P. (2016) Finnish schools and the global education reform movement, in J. Evers and R. Kneyber (eds) *Flip the System: Changing Education from the Ground Up*, 162–74. Abingdon: Routledge.

Sedova, K. and Navratilova, J. (2020) Silent students and the patterns of their participation in classroom talk, *Journal of the Learning Sciences*, 29(4–5): 681–716.

Sedova, K., Sedlacek, M., Svaricek, R. et al. (2019) Do those who talk more learn more? The relationship between student classroom talk and student achievement, *Learning and Instruction*, 63: 101217.

Segal, A. and Lefstein, A. (2016). Exuberant, voiceless participation: an unintended consequence of dialogic sensibilities? Contribution to a special issue on International Perspectives on Dialogic Theory and Practice, edited by Sue Brindley, Mary Juzwik and Alison Whitehurst. *L1-Educational Studies in Language and Literature*, 16: 1–19.

Shulman, L. and Wilson, S. (2004). *The Wisdom of Practice: Essays on Teaching, Learning, and Learning to Teach*. San Francisco, CA: Jossey-Bass.

Sinclair, J. and Coulthard, R. (1975) *Towards an Analysis of Discourse: The English Used by Teachers and Pupils*. Oxford: Oxford University Press.

Smith, F., Hardman, F., Wall, K. and Mroz, M. (2004) Interactive whole class teaching in the National Literacy and Numeracy Strategies, *British Educational Research Journal*, 30(3): 395–411.

Snell, J. and Lefstein, A. (2018) 'Low ability', participation and identity in dialogic pedagogy, *American Educational Research Journal*, 55(1): 40–78.

Snowling, M., Hulme, C., Bailey, A. et al. (2011) *Better Communication Research Programme: Language and Literacy Attainment of Pupils during Early Years and through KS2: Does teacher assessment at five provide a valid measure of children's current and future educational attainments?* Department for Education Research Brief 172a. Available at: https://files.eric.ed.gov/fulltext/ED526910.pdf (accessed 18 April 2022).

Solomon, Y. and Lewin, C. (2016) Measuring 'progress': performativity as both driver and constraint in school innovation, *Journal of Education Policy*, 31(2): 226–38.

Sun, J., Anderson, R., Lin, T. and Morris, J. (2015) Social and cognitive development during collaborative reasoning, in L. Resnick, C. Asterhan and S. Clarke (eds) *Socializing Intelligence Through Academic Talk and Dialogue*, 63–75. Washington, DC: American Educational Research Association.

Sutton Trust (2012) *Social Mobility and Education Gaps in the Four Major Anglophone Countries: Research Findings for the Social Mobility Summit*. Available at: https://www.suttontrust.com/our-research/social-mobility-education-gaps-four-major-anglophone-countries-research-findings-social-mobility-summit-london-2012/ (accessed 18 April 2022).

Sweller, J. (2016) Working memory, long-term memory and instructional design, *Journal of Applied Research in Memory and Cognition*, 5: 360–67.

Tan, C. (2019) Parental responses to education reform in Singapore, Shanghai and Hong King, *Asia Pacific Education Review*, 20: 91–9.

Teo, P. (2016) Exploring the dialogic space in teaching: a study of teacher talk in the pre-university classroom in Singapore, *Teaching and Teacher Education*, 56: 47–60.

Topping, K. and Trickey, S. (2014) The role of dialog in philosophy for children, *International Journal of Educational Research*, 63: 69–78.

Trickey, S. and Topping, K. (2004) 'Philosophy for children': a systematic review, *Research Papers in Education*, 19(3): 365–80.

T-SEDA Collective (2021) *Teacher Scheme for Educational Dialogue Analysis (T-SEDA) v.8a resource pack*. University of Cambridge. Available at: http://bit.ly/T-SEDA (accessed 18 April 2022).

UNICEF (1990) *The United Nations Convention on the Rights of the Child*. Available at: www.unicef.org.uk/what-we-do/un-convention-child-rights/ (accessed 18 April 2022).

Vaish, V. (2008) Interactional patterns in Singapore's English classrooms, *Linguistics and Education*, 19(4): 366–77.

Van de Pol, J., Volman, M. and Beishuizen, J. (2010) Scaffolding in teacher–student interaction: a decade of research, *Educational Psychology Review*, 22: 271–96.

Van der Wilt, F., van Kruistrum, C., van der Veen, C. et al. (2016) Gender differences in the relationship between oral communicative competence and peer rejection: an explorative study in early childhood education, *European Early Childhood Education Research Journal*, 24(6): 807–17.

Visible Learning (2018) *Hattie Ranking: 252 Influences and Effect Sizes Related to Student Achievement*. Available at: https://visible-learning.org/hattie-ranking-influences-effect-sizes-learning-achievement/ (accessed 18 April 2022).

Voice 21 (2019) *The Oracy Benchmarks*. Available at: https://voice21.org/wp-content/uploads/2019/10/Benchmarks-report-Digital.pdf (accessed 18 April 2022).

Voice 21 (2020a) *The Oracy Framework*. Available at: https://voice21.org/wp-content/uploads/2022/04/The-Oracy-Framework-2021.pdf (accessed 18 April 2022).

Voice 21 (2020b) *3 tips for developing an oracy rich approach to online learning*. Available at: https://voice21.org/3-tips-for-developing-an-oracy-rich-approach-to-online-learning/ (accessed 18 April 2022).

Vygotsky, L. (1978) *Mind in Society: The Development of Higher Psychological Processes*. Boston, MA: Harvard University Press.

Warwick, P., Cook, V., Vrikki, M. et al. (2020) Realising 'dialogic intentions' when working with a microblogging tool in secondary school classrooms, *Learning, Culture and Social Interaction*, 24: 100376.

Webb, N., Franke, M., Ing, M. et al. (2014) Engaging with others' mathematical ideas: interrelationships among student participation, teachers' instructional practices and learning, *International Journal of Educational Research*, 63: 79–93.

Webb, P., Whitlow, J. and Venter, D. (2017) From exploratory talk to abstract reasoning: a case for far transfer?, *Educational Psychology Review*, 29: 565–81.

Wegerif, R. (2007) *Dialogic Teaching and Technology*. New York: Springer.

Wegerif, R. (2010) *Mind Expanding: Teaching for Thinking and Creativity in Primary Education*. Maidenhead: Open University Press.

Wegerif, R. (2020) *Oracy as the Vaccine against Truth Decay*. Available at: https://oracy-cambridge.org/oracy-vaccine-truth-decay/ (accessed 18 April 2022).

Wegerif, R. and Dawes, L. (2004) *Thinking and Learning with ICT: Raising Achievement in Primary Classrooms*. Abingdon: Routledge.

Wells, G. and Arauz, R. (2006) Dialogue in the classroom, *Journal of the Learning Sciences*, 15(3): 379–428.

Wertsch, J. (2008) From social interaction to higher psychological processes: a clarification and application of Vygotsky's theory, *Human Development*, 51: 66–79.

Wilkinson, A. (1965) The concept of oracy, *English in Education*, 2(A2): 3–5.

Willingham, D. (2007) Critical thinking: why is it so hard to teach?, *American Educator*, Summer 2007: 8–19.

Wood, D. (1992) Teaching talk, in K. Norman (ed.) *Thinking Voices: The Work of the National Oracy Project*, 203–14. London: Hodder and Stoughton.

Wood, D., Bruner, J. and Ross, G. (1976) The role of tutoring in problem solving, *Journal of Child Psychiatry*, 17: 89–100.

Wrigley, T. (2018) The power of 'evidence': reliable science or a set of blunt tools?, *British Educational Research Journal*, 44(3): 359–76.

Yang, Y. (2016) Lessons learnt from contextualising a UK teaching thinking program in a conventional Chinese classroom, *Thinking Skills and Creativity*, 19: 198–209.

Zepeda, C., Hlutkowsky, C., Partika, A. and Nokes-Malach, T. (2019) Identifying teachers' supports of metacognition through classroom talk and its relation to growth in conceptual learning, *Journal of Educational Psychology*, 111(3): 522–41.

Index